W9-AER-934

the
pantry

the
pantry
ITS HISTORY AND MODERN USES

BY CATHERINE SEIBERLING POND

GIBBS
P
SMITH

Gibbs Smith, Publisher
TO ENRICH AND INSPIRE HUMANKIND

Salt Lake City | Charleston | Santa Fe | Santa Barbara

First Edition
11 10 09 08 07   5 4 3 2 1

Text © 2007 Catherine Seiberling Pond
Photograph credits on page 95

Published by
Gibbs Smith, Publisher
P.O. Box 667
Layton, Utah 84041

Orders: 1.800.835.4993
www.gibbs-smith.com

Designed by m:GraphicDesign
Printed and bound in Hong Kong

Library of Congress Cataloging-in-Publication Data

Pond, Catherine Seiberling.
The pantry / Catherine Seiberling Pond. —1st ed.
p. cm.
Includes bibliographical references.
ISBN-13: 978-1-4236-0004-6
ISBN-10: 1-4236-0004-5

1. Kitchens—History. 2. Kitchens—Design and construction. I. Title.

TX653.P585 2007
643′.3—dc22

2006022208

front cover: An assembled collection of vintage objects and everyday kitchen items will liven a pantry from any era. Photo courtesy of F & E Schmidt Photography.

page 2: Secret Cupboards: Old closets with shelves found in many historic homes were often early pantries and make ideal spaces to display collections. Here is an open cupboard with vintage kitchen items from the 1930s, as well as foodstuffs.

page 8: Dainty shelf paper accents this late-nineteenth-century pantry.

back cover: A view of the two original pantries that flank an old Hoosier in the kitchen of this 1890 home. Recently restored to the period, the pantries only needed a new coat of paint.

*To my dear Grandpa Sei (James Penfield Seiberling) (1898–1982)
and beloved Dad (James Henry Seiberling) (1936–2002),
who both always knew I would write.*

"How few rooms impress us so deeply that they become a part of our lives in memory of influence. . . . We need rooms which hold out warm, inviting arms, rooms into which we can go and feel the atmosphere wrap us around with soothing and content. There must be rooms which cool for us the fevered strain of life, or by some flash of beauty mingled with the walls and chairs stir us to be more than what we were when we entered that room. . . . Remembered rooms speak to us in the low tireless tones of beauty whose impress can never be forgotten." [1]

—Lydia Lion Roberts

facing: A preserved nineteenth-century pantry from an 1830s farmhouse in Upstate New York is now furnished with period antiques. The owners are fortunate to have an original 1874 journal kept by Helen Tripp, then nineteen years old. "We cleaned the large pantry and scoured the tin," she wrote on May 12, and on the following day, Helen related, "We cleaned the little pantry and part of the back kitchen." Household journals kept by women often recorded pantry-related tasks.

CONTENTS

"She led me to her kitchen, flung wide the pantry door, and there on the lower shelf lay an open book with a long ribbon marker. 'That part of the shelf is dedicated to my book,' she explained. 'Once I had a teacher who said, "Dorothy, if you love life, you'll never squander your time, for time is the stuff that life is made of."' . . . I've always remembered this teacher's words. There are so many things I want to know, and so little time from the baking, scrubbing and other daily tasks. Yet during my day there are many spare minutes. Whenever I can, I use them in reading my book on the pantry shelf. In all these years I haven't served many burned dishes."[2]

—Beatrice Wilson, "The Book on the Pantry Shelf," *Farmer's Wife*

IN THE PANTRY

Pantry—the crisp, even tidy, sound of the word conveys a sense of order and "a place for everything and everything in its place." Perhaps the origin of that well-worn cliché comes from *The Practical Housekeeper*, written by Mrs. Elizabeth Ellet in 1857: "Let there be a place for every article, and when not in use let every article be in its place."

Pantries harbor a nostalgic whiff of our domestic past. Like the attic of an old house, filled with the stuff and chaff of generations, pantries hold the staples and extra things from our kitchens and dining rooms. From early America, throughout the broad stretch of nineteenth-century building styles, and well into the twentieth century, the pantry evolved along with the many socioeconomic and design changes in the American home. As well as storage and preparation space, a butler's pantry during the Victorian era was a buffer between the domestic service arena of the kitchen and the murmur of a full-course dinner party. Meanwhile, the self-sufficient farmhouse had pantries and a warren of workrooms for preparing a vast amount of food to eat and store. There is a universal quality to the food pantry and cellar storeroom—they are symbolic of a plentiful simplicity dependent on what we "put up" from our own place and not what we purchased at a store.

When I was eleven I bought my first cookbook, *The New England Butt'ry Shelf Cookbook*, by Mary Mason Campbell. While drawn to the book because of its diminutive size, nostalgic watercolor illustrations by Tasha Tudor, and traditional New England recipes, it was the title that especially appealed—*what was a butt'ry?* I thought. It sounded old-fashioned and certainly like it came from old New England, a place I loved to visit each summer when we stayed with my grandparents in their 1792 farmhouse. Meanwhile, back in Ohio, my paternal grandparents had a huge 1920s-era serving pantry where colorful glassware and gold-trimmed sets of china shimmered behind tall glass cabinets awaiting the next holiday gathering. Usually on the counter was a tin full of cutout ginger cookies from an old German family recipe—I can still smell and taste them in my mind.

Pantries can be a part of our longings for Grandmother's kitchen or a place of memories. Nearly everyone has a pantry memory or reference to share. One friend describes rummaging with her cousins through her grandparents' series of pantries at their grand hilltop summer estate and making instant gelatins that they "attempted to whip up into elegant desserts."

"I swear I could *live* in a pantry and be perfectly content," said another fellow pantry aficionado and friend. "I don't know what it is about them but they remind me of my favorite Chip and Dale cartoon when I was really little. They lived in a walnut that had little shelves with little jars and nuts. It was so cozy." Another woman, as a little girl, liked to sleep in the pantry in her family home along with her dog.

A pantry can invoke all manner of pleasant things—visual delights, memories of taste and smell, perhaps even security and comfort. After a long century of pantry decline, many American households are once again returning to the pantry to store their foodstuffs, dishes, unusual collections, and memories of their own making. This book offers ideas and design inspiration for those who wish to create or restore a pantry and for those interested in the domestic history and evolution of American kitchens. ✿

A pantry, like this one from the early 1900s, can be an ancillary space for the kitchen as well as a nostalgic place for domestic memory.

ACKNOWLEDGMENTS

Nothing is ever a solitary achievement. I am especially grateful to my editors, Madge Baird and Katie Newbold, and to everyone at Gibbs Smith, Publisher, who provided a delightful first experience in the book world. Patty Poore, editor at *Old-House Interiors*, first published my article on pantries and continues to offer me writing opportunities for which I am thankful. I appreciate, as always, the time and care from the staff at Stan Hywet Hall & Gardens: special thanks to staff members Christine Montague, Laurie Gilles, and Mark Heppner.

I want to thank all of the "pantry people" who shared their own pantries or pantry memories or told me about others: Steve Butterweck, John Carpenter, Harriet Chapman, Justine Cook, Lucy and Shirley Davison, Judy Johnson, Rosemary Mack, Edie Powell, Peter and Ann Sawyer, Sister Frances Carr, Brother Arnold Hadd, and the United Society of Shakers in Sabbathday Lake, Maine, and others who let us into their homes to photograph—thank you! For all of my blogsite readers at inthepantry.blogspot.com, I appreciate your reading and sharing of my interests in both the minutiae and mundane of domestic life and the power of place.

My friend Susan Daley always offers much support and guidance in every realm—this time for my book proposal and throughout the writing process. I am honored to have the exquisite interior photography of Susan Daley and Steve Gross in this book. Their shared sense of the past—and way of seeing—is something I admire and embrace, almost as much as their friendship. Their intrinsic sense of style is an inspiration.

I could not have even had the time to think about pantries if it were not for my husband, Temple Pond. His ability to take on domestic tasks, to soothe and feed our three children, and to drive them off in three different directions—all in a single bound and without complaint—allows me to write. His love, support, and enthusiasm means everything to me, and after ten years of marriage (and thirty plus in each other's worlds) we are a true team. To our children—Addie, Henry, and Eli—I appreciate your patience and understanding throughout the many stretches of "Mommy Is on the Computer Again." As rewarding as writing can be, it will never compare to how blessed I am to be your mother. And thanks and love to my mother—always.

THE EARLY AMERICAN PANTRY

LARDERS, BUTT'RIES, AND STOREROOMS

Early American pantries were an outgrowth of food storage use in attics, cellars, and butteries (small rooms pronounced *butt'ries*). Several hundred years before the canning or freezing processes were discovered, these cooler rooms adjacent to the kitchen were filled with crocks of pickled fruits and vegetables, molasses, salt, salted beef or pork, and leftover provisions, like a pot of unfinished beans or baked Indian pudding. Early pantries were unheated, dry areas of the home that became the provisional storage areas of the colonial household up and down the Eastern seaboard.

Most colonial homes were built facing south to maximize light and warmth. Within the added lean-to of the seventeenth-century house was a buttery at one end of the kitchen, a small, warm bedroom or additional storeroom at the other end, and a small attic above, which formed the salt-box look of the roof and became additional food-storage space for the kitchen.

Adjacent to the combined kitchen and living area—where the hearth was central to most domestic operations like cooking, candle making, dyeing, and home comfort—early butteries or pantries were primitively fashioned storage areas with open, unpainted shelves and barrels for flour, sugar, and other provisions kept below. Butter churning, cheese pressing, bread making, and other preparations took place in the pantry with the lower shelves doubling as counter space. A window for ventilation and light was also essential. The name *buttery* comes not from the butter and dairy products kept there but from the butts of barrels that lined the floor.

Most colonial homes utilized their attics and cellars for additional food storage and drying, especially as they evolved

facing: The simple pine shelving in this restored early pantry (or buttery) now displays the homeowner's period antiques. The spare simplicity of the room is typical of the period.

in size by the end of the eighteenth century. At this time it was not unusual to find homes with a pantry and a buttery (as overflow), a smoking room (often incorporated into the chimney base), a shed, a shed chamber, an attic or a garret, a milk room, and a cellar.

The colonial kitchen was as aromatic as it was colorful: redolent with smells from stews cooked on the open fire, breads and beans and puddings baking in the beehive oven, freshly ground spices, or perhaps meat roasting in the tin kitchen or on a spit. Other smells were of kitchen industry: at different times, tallow was kept warm for candles or animal fat was rendered for soap. At the hearth, wool was also dyed before later being spun

and woven into cloth, and water was boiled for seasonal laundering and the occasional bath. In the spring, sap was boiled down in the large kettle to make maple syrup, just as it was used throughout the year for preserves and fruit butters. Hasty pudding, a form of mush made from cornmeal, was a staple of early New Englanders and was kept warm over the fire throughout the day. The colonial kitchen was also unintentionally decorous in the herbs and strings of peppers, pumpkins, and apples hung to dry along the beams. A big table—or quite literally a narrow plank in earlier homes—was used for eating and working.

Regularly used iron or tin implements were stored around the hearth, but most items were stored in the buttery, along with

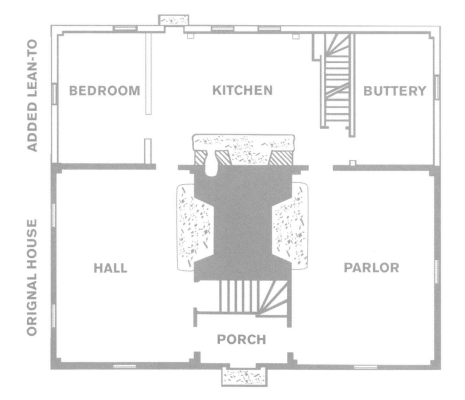

left: This seventeenth-century house plan displays a typical configuration that would predominate in American domestic architecture for over two centuries. An added lean-to, providing a saltbox roof, housed a separate kitchen and adjacent rooms, including a buttery.

facing: The pantry area at the Zadock Pratt House in Prattsville, New York, was called the "cold room." It was on the north side of the house, adjacent to the kitchen herb garden.

AMERICA'S OLDEST INTACT PANTRY?

The Theron Boyd Homestead in Hartford, Vermont, may well have the oldest, most intact pantry in the United States. This large Georgian farmhouse built in 1786 and now managed by the Vermont Division for Historic Preservation has been virtually untouched with few, if any, architectural changes or modern improvements. The house was last occupied in 1986, and a cast-iron sink with running water was the only concession to modern life. In the northwest corner of the main house, just off the kitchen, a good-sized pantry—likely painted once and now worn to its original wood—has shelves, large work counters, and a window. Paint analysis of one early intact layer reveals that this room has never been altered or renovated. The hand-wrought nails used in the carpentry also support that evidence. Unusual for such a utilitarian space, many of the shelves have decoratively scalloped brackets.

Meanwhile, in the southwest corner of the cellar, a brick-lined storeroom lies two feet below the rest of the cellar with wooden shelving brackets inserted along the brick walls where food and jars would have been stored. The barrel-vaulted chimney base was also used for food storage and another area was used for a root cellar.

This pantry dates back to 1786 and is likely the best example of an unaltered Early American pantry. Many of the shelves have decoratively scalloped brackets, which is unusual for such a utilitarian space.

"On a hot day in Virginia, I know of nothing more comforting than a fine, spiced pickle, brought up trout-like from the sparkling depths of that aromatic jar below stairs in Aunt Sally's cellar."

—*Thomas Jefferson*

a vast supply of homemade woodenware, including covered pantry boxes for spices and dried goods, firkins and barrels for larger supplies, bowls, water buckets, ladles, spoons, and early mortars and pestles. Later on in the seventeenth century, a hutch or dresser in the kitchen may have kept pewter plates and tankards, wooden trenchers, or the woman's best imported china. Throughout the seventeenth and eighteenth centuries there was little evolution in the kitchen realm—only in foodstuffs and available implements.

Since the American Centennial in 1876, the colonial hearth has been persistently romanticized, but the realities are far grittier: the open fire was a dangerous place to tend in long skirts and to keep children from; the grease of winter cooking would have lingered long in smell and presence; and the endless work routines of the colonial housewife rarely gave one pause to enjoy the fire. Yet, the hearth was the center of the home, providing warmth, comfort, sustenance, and winter light by which to knit or darn. Unlike the later Victorian kitchen,

above: A nostalgic Victorian image of an early American housewife in her larder or buttery.

right: This New England cupboard (c. 1816) is unusual because it is an early example of a built-in cabinet and would have been used as a kind of pantry. Today it displays a collection of yellowware made in America during the late nineteenth and early twentieth centuries.

ENGLISH PROTOTYPES

Pantry and larder are often synonymous terms, especially in England. In the Middle Ages foodstuffs were stored in bulk to accommodate large castle dinners and the inevitability of being under siege for long stretches. The larder was a cool room or cellar for storing meats and spoilable foods; meats were originally stored in barrels or crocks of rendered lard, hence the name. Dried or smoked meats were stored in an attic or drier storage area. Due to the varying food-storage needs, a *wet larder* and a *dry larder* were invented. The wet larder was a place to store uncooked meat, game, vegetables, and fruits, while the dry larder held dried fruit, grains, and cheeses. Meanwhile, a buttery was originally a storeroom for large barrels, or "butts," of beer, ale, and large provisions. In castles with great halls, the nobility ate at one end, on the dais raised above the rest of the room, and on the opposite wall was a screen that divided the great hall from the corridor that led to the pantry and buttery, where servants carried food back and forth to the diners.

The word *pantry* and related words like *pantry man* and *pannier* are derived from the Latin word for bread, *panis*. The French stored their bread in a bread cupboard called a *paneterie*. A *pantler* was the servant in charge of serving the bread and slicing it for the table. He was regarded as a person of lesser nobility, though the position became prestigious for a servant, as bread was considered a staple of the medieval dinner. Finely carved cupboards held bread especially kept for the table. Victorian England would retain the many workrooms, storerooms, and larders in its larger homes and estates, as in the Middle Ages, while almost all smaller dwellings, as in America, had a kitchen pantry (or larder) and a butler's pantry.

which was relegated to the back of the house or ell—"something that was not talked about nor exhibited with pride"[1] because only servants used this space in more prosperous homes—the colonial kitchen was truly the center of things, the place where the family gathered to do their tasks and also to dine.

Early New Englanders had corn, fish, and game as their primary foodstuffs. Pumpkins, or *pompions*, were also a staple as they were easy to grow, store, and prepare. Potatoes, parsnips, carrots, peas, turnips, and beans were also grown by early settlers. Grapes, cranberries, blueberries, and strawberries all grew wild, and apple orchards were planted, soon followed by pear and quince. Apple slices, like pumpkins, were hung to dry on string in attics or garrets. Rye grew more easily than wheat at first and, along with corn, was a staple in breads. Ale, rum, and cider rounded out the foodstuffs and were stored in barrels in the cellar or storeroom. Dairying began as cows became more prevalent, and, by the eighteenth century, milk, cheese, and butter were staples of the American diet.

In the mid-twentieth century, rumor and speculation existed about an unusual lazy-Susan-type structure in a preserve closet or kitchen-storage area of an old farmhouse in northeastern Massachusetts. The contraption was found and documented by the American Institute of Architects in the early 1940s, who were "allowed to look through a doorway into an enclosed, nearly square space, much cluttered with old packages, cartons, bottles and crocks, having

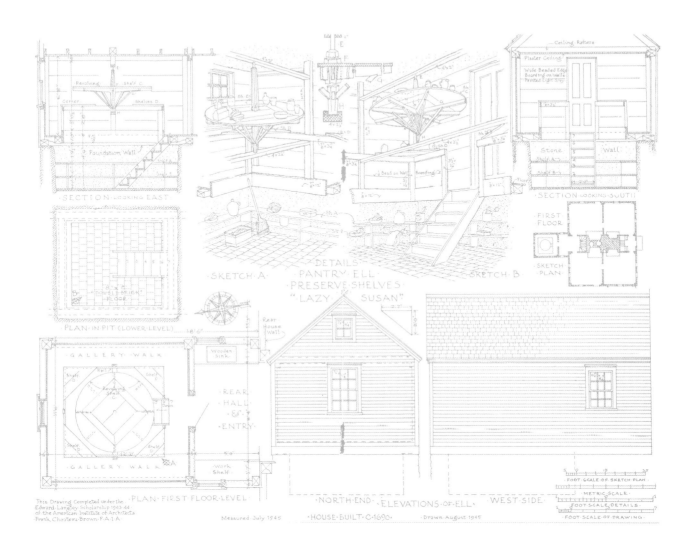

SECTION · LOOKING · EAST

Revolving · Shelf · C
Corner · Shelves · D
Foundation Wall

SKETCH · A ·

DETAILS
PANTRY · ELL ·
PRESERVE · SHELVES ·
" LAZY · SUSAN "

SKETCH · B ·

SECTION · LOOKING · SOUTH

Ceiling · Rafters
Plaster Ceiling
Wide Beaded Edge
Boarding · on · Walls
Painted Light Grey
Stone Wall
Shelf · A ·
Shelf · B ·

FIRST
FLOOR

SKETCH ·
PLAN ·

PLAN · IN · PIT · (LOWER · LEVEL)

Double · Brick ·
FLOOR

GALLERY · WALK ·
Revolving · Shelf ·
GALLERY · WALK ·

PLAN · FIRST · FLOOR · LEVEL ·

This Drawing Completed under the
Edward · Langley · Scholarship 1943-44
of the American Institute of Architects
Frank · Chouteau · Brown · F · A · I · A ·

Rear
House
Wall
Wooden Sink

· REAR ·
· HALL ·
· & ·
· ENTRY ·

Work
Shelf

Measured · July · 1945

· NORTH · END · ELEVATIONS · OF · ELL · WEST · SIDE ·
· HOUSE · BUILT · C · 1690 ·   · Drawn · August · 1945 ·

FOOT · SCALE · OF · SKETCH · PLAN ·
METRIC · SCALE ·
FOOT · SCALE · DETAILS ·
FOOT · SCALE · OF · DRAWING ·

This mid-twentieth-century architectural drawing documents the lazy
Susan contraption as found in an ell attached to an Early American New
England farmhouse. It was specifically built as a cold food–storage room.

A Federal-style pantry appears in the doorway beyond the dining room
at Constable Hall (1819).

a wooden walk around an open pit, over the middle of which was a large circular turning shelf, set about a central pivot, with two or more 'stories.'"[2] The large New England house, which dated from 1690, had a small ell attached to the middle of its rear elevation. The exact location was never revealed in the article, and it is unknown whether the house and its unusual pantry still exist today.

In the southern climates, it was not unusual for early homes and plantations to have separate outdoor structures for cooking, smoking meats, and various tasks. At Mount Vernon, George and Martha Washington's late-eighteenth-century Virginia estate, thirty separate small structures on the plantation, were associated with domestic life. In addition to a kitchen connected to the main house by an arcade, there was a storehouse, smokehouse, salt house, milk house, springhouse, butler's house, and even the luxury of an icehouse. Other buildings housed domestic tasks or servants. According to accounts, all of these buildings were visited each day by Martha Washington and a woman who carried the key basket (containing all of the keys to plantation buildings). Life at Mount Vernon, as it was with other prosperous homes, plantations, and later farmsteads across the country, was a well-oiled domestic engine:

> All the principal food was furnished by the plantation. Vegetables were raised in profusion in the garden. The butter was made in the dairy, and milk and cream was kept in the cool springhouse near by. Turkeys and chickens were raised on the farm, barrels of sugar were in the pantry, brown sugar to be used by the slaves and for cooking, and lump sugar for the mistress's table.[3]

Other early kitchens—such as those of the Dutch settlers in New York and English settlers in Virginia had different kitchen designs and contents than their New England neighbors. Dutch kitchens generally had large, heavy cupboards for food and implement storage and were often in the cellar or a separate building with adjacent storerooms or milk rooms that contained their supplies and work utensils. Other early settlers—German, Swedish, and Irish—brought their own unique imprints on the evolution of the Early American kitchen. Eventually, with the westward expansion across the country,

"*The kitchen in all the farmhouses of all the colonies was the most cheerful, homelike, and picturesque room in the house.... The ears of corn were often piled into the attic until the floor was a foot deep with them. I once entered an ell bedroom in a Massachusetts farmhouse where the walls, rafters, and four-post bedstead were hung solid with ears of yellow corn, which truly 'made sunshine in a shady place.'"[4]*
—Alice Morse Earle, Home Life in Colonial Days

EARLY AMERICAN PANTRY STYLE

❀ USE OPEN WOOD SHELVES, OFTEN
STAINED OR PAINTED WITH MILK
PAINT.

❀ DISPLAY EARLY COLLECTIONS OF
WOODENWARE, TINWARE, AND
CROCKERY.

❀ PLACE BASKETS OR LARGE
BARRELS ON THE FLOOR
UNDERNEATH SHELVING.

❀ HANG HERBS OR BUNCHES OF
FLOWERS TO DRY.

❀ PUT SEASONAL FRUITS AND
SQUASHES IN BASKETS OR BOWLS.

❀ KEEP MODERN APPLIANCES OR
CANNED GOODS IN CABINETS
BELOW SHELVING.

primitive one-room cabins gave way to an architectural and domestic evolution that by the twentieth century had become more uniform—and efficient—across the country. But in those Early American kitchens are the prototypes for generations of cooking, food storage, and pantries that would not really alter in any great way for several centuries. ❀

facing page: Early pantries, like their adjacent colonial kitchens, were multifunctional spaces. This pantry from the early 1800s also features a soapstone sink.

THE
FARMHOUSE
PANTRY

WORKROOMS OF SELF-SUFFICIENCY

The farmhouse pantry was an extension of Early American prototypes that never went away, evolving from the buttery into a patterning of task-specific workrooms and storage areas such as cellars, dairies, washrooms, springhouses, and summer kitchens that existed well into the twentieth century. Farmhouses were domestic mechanisms of self-sufficiency. With their own growth and prosperity, the American farm developed specialized rooms for various tasks while the pantry remained an integral part of the household and farmyard enterprise.

A farmhouse pantry and its related rooms, acting as a genuine storehouse for the self-sufficient farmwife, were an essential component of the farm. Various storerooms—in the cellar or ell—provided extended areas to keep canned goods, preserves, and all manner of foodstuffs. As dining generally took place in the farm kitchen, butler's pantries were primarily found in urban and suburban homes except in the most up-to-date and prosperous of farm homes.

It is more often the farmhouse pantry that is conjured when Grandmother's pantry is mentioned. As early as the late nineteenth century, domestic writers and others were waxing nostalgic about Grandmother's kitchen of yesteryear: "Oh, that kitchen of the olden times, the old, clean, roomy New England kitchen!—who that has breakfasted, dined, and supped in one has not cheery visions of its thrift, its warmth, its coolness? . . . Let us not forget our grandmothers' kitchens!"[1] Yet the farm kitchen still persisted in some areas of the country throughout the twentieth century.

There are countless American memoirs of growing up on a farm, and invariably, each one includes a kitchen or pantry

facing: This Hoosier cabinet at the Chapman Hotel in North Blenheim, New York, served as a kind of pantry and is also an iconic symbol of the farmhouse kitchen.

"Adelaide, Mate, and my mother, all veterans in the art of country cooking, moved from 'butt'ry' to table to stove to table to 'butt'ry,' back and forth, forward and back, around and past each other like human shuttles weaving a pattern which had form, color, flavor, and a fourth quality, impalpable but memorably significant, that of odor. Odors piquant with spice as ginger-molasses cookies came from the oven, sheet after sheet, their fat bellies dented, navel-like, with a raisin plumped by heat. Odor of pumpkin being stewed down in an iron kettle, leafily sweet . . . odors presaging others still more poignant that would follow later."[2]

—*Della T. Lutes*

memory. There is something about a farm kitchen with its accompanying pantry that brings about a nostalgic longing for another time. Perhaps it is the idea of others—like a beloved mother or grandmother and their daughters—providing all of the food on a farm, when in reality it was hard work. Regardless, the romance of past pantries lingers over the many sensory experiences found in and around a farm kitchen. Unlike later kitchens, which would be relegated as servant-run workrooms or efficient laboratories, the farm kitchen has always been the center of the home. Farm kitchens prevailed well into the twentieth century in rural America but have now become almost as forsaken as the pantry. 🏵

A nostalgic, early-twentieth-century image of preserving—something every farmwife did by necessity.

A worktable such as this, found at the Chapman Hotel in North
Blenheim, New York, was essential to any kitchen or pantry.

AN ORIGINAL FARMHOUSE PANTRY

In a 1790s New England farmhouse there is a perfectly preserved pantry from the early twentieth century. Now a summer home in Dublin, New Hampshire, the house was reconstructed in the Federal style after a fire in the early 1900s burned the original house and barn to the foundations. The house, bought in 1929 by Mrs. Mabel Bremer from Boston, was named "Yonder Farm"; she later sold the house in the mid-1930s to its current family, now in their third generation of occupancy. The pantry dates to the 1908–09 rebuilding of the house and retains its original robin's egg blue paint, a popular utilitarian paint choice of the period. Storing an eclectic cache of family china, crockery, and glassware, the walk-through pantry between kitchen and dining room was originally used for both food and dishes. Another unique feature of this pantry-kitchen complex is an adjacent laundry room, also original to 1908–09. With its ample cupboard storage and a large soapstone sink, it is, in essence, a laundry pantry. 🌸

right, top: A southern-facing window above a handy work sink, provides warmth, light, and ventilation to this pantry space.

right, bottom: The laundry room at Yonder Farm, on the other side of the kitchen near the barn, is a typical farmhouse workroom with its divided soapstone sink and ample storage.

facing: Bead board was a popular choice for utilitarian spaces and farmhouse kitchens. A 1920s Colonial Revival embellishment can be found in the decorative column between the cabinet and countertop.

FARMHOUSE PANTRY TERMS

Buttery or Butt'ry
A New England term taken from the Medieval English usage of the word: a cool, dry place for foodstuffs—often an overflow of the kitchen pantry.

Cellar or Root Cellar
No farmhouse was without a cellar for additional food storage. The cellar kept preserves, canned goods, pickle vats, salt pork, and preserved meats cool, dry, and temperate throughout the year.

Milk House or Milk Room
This important dairy room where cheese and butter were prepared was often incorporated into the farm kitchen for ease of access and sanitary reasons. Eventually, the milk room became either a separate farm structure or part of the barn.

Springhouse
The springhouse was built over a cold, flowing spring, often channeled into a sluiceway or flanked by flat rocks on which to place foodstuffs. The room was cold and the perfect place to store dairy goods and other perishable items.

Summer Kitchen
Summer kitchens, particularly in New England but often in other parts of the country, were usually attached to the north of the main house or in an ell between the shed and main barn. Here food was prepared in summer in an area where heat and smells could be kept away from the main house. In the South, kitchens were built in separate buildings for this purpose.

above: A cool corner in an Amish summer kitchen, used for canning in the hot summer months. The room now serves as a small bakery at the Yonder farmhouse in Holmes County, Ohio.

facing: The early-twentieth-century pantry at Yonder Farm embodies the essence of country style with its plain construction and utilitarian green paint. Through the door, beyond, is the original farmhouse kitchen.

PUTTING FOOD BY

The Amish farmwife, in her almost total self-sufficiency, is a fine modern example of how American women used to exist on farms. Farmwives of the past began to embrace the conveniences afforded to them in grocery stores and with modern utilities and appliances. Mormons, too, have long advocated having a storeroom with a year's supply of saved foodstuffs and provisions. People in communes and those in the back-to-the-land movement were also avid food pre-servers. Where canning was once a necessity on the farm, especially before freezers were available, it now continues as a pleasant pastime for some.

The cellar, as well as the pantry, became an important place for food storage on the farm. Haydn S. Pearson describes the abundance of the harvest stored in glass jars in the farmhouse cellar of his boyhood:

Our farm cellar was a wonderful place. All sum-mer long mother canned and preserved. There was a long wide shelf, suspended from the floor timbers that ran most of the length of the cellar. On this were jars of colorful cherries, blueber-ries, and raspberries. There were jars of string beans, peas, and corn. In cupboards along the south wall were scores of jars of jellies and jams, pickles, and preserved plums. When you went downstairs to the cellar, the colors of the fruits and jellies made an appealing picture in the golden lantern light. . . . Mother's pickled crab apples were a special favorite. They were beau-tifully colored miniature apples, pickled in a just-right brine, and each apple with its stem so you could manipulate it in accord with the tenets of gracious living.[3]

left: Ball, as well as other canning supply com-panies, appealed to the farmwife and all women to preserve food as part of the war effort.

above: Canning and pickling all manner of vegetables and fruits was a popular pastime for many and a necessity for others. This set of typed recipes was passed along through a New England family.

facing: The Florida farmhouse pantry of Marjorie Kinnan Rawlings in Cross Creek, where the author moved in 1928. She wrote in *Cross Creek Cookery:* "I always keep on hand in the pantry cans of sliced or halves of peaches, and a good shortcake may be made on a moment's notice."[4]

For several decades, Lucy Davison has put up the bounty from the garden at the New England farm she shares with her husband, Shirley, 87. Their farmhouse has a long, narrow pantry with shelves and a large workspace in front of a sunny window. "I love a pantry," Lucy says. "I do my baking preparations in there because we entertain in the kitchen—you just leave the bread and the old milk cup and dirty bowls. You can take off your apron and close the door." Their kitchen has a reliable Glendale stove where she does her extensive canning: tomatoes, pickles, all kinds of jams and jellies.

"*Our list of fall fruits is completed; the hard, back-breaking work is at an end, and we feel as if—well, we never wanted to see or taste jelly again. But there are few of us who do not in time regain an appetite for these dainty relishes, and who do not, after a rest, enjoy viewing the array upon our pantry shelves.*"[5]

—Annie Curd

My Mother's Cooky Jar

In a dim old country pantry where the light just sifted through,
Where they kept the pies and spices and the jam and honey, too,
Where the air is always fragrant with the smell of things to eat,
And the coolness was a refuge from the burning summer heat, —
It was there I used to find it, when I went to help myself, —
That old cooky jar a-setting underneath the pantry shelf.
Talk of manna straight from heaven! Why, it isn't on a par
With those good old-fashioned cookies from my mother's cooky jar.

I am sick of fancy cooking; I am weary of the ways
Of the butler and the waiters. Give me back my boyhood days!
Give me back the good old kitchen, with its roominess and light,
Where the farm hands did their "sparking" almost every winter night!
Give me back my boyhood hunger and the things my mother made!
Give me back that well-filled pantry where I used to make a raid!
Take me back, as though forgetting all the years which mark and mar—
Let me taste once more the cookies from mother's cooky jar![6]

—from My Mother's Cooky Jar *by A. B. Braley*

THE FARMHOUSE BUTT'RY

"City people used to have pantries," begins Mary Mason Campbell in her romantic homage to the New England pantry in *The Butt'ry Shelf Cookbook.* "The country counterpart of the pantry was called a 'butt'ry.' In occasional hidden corners of New England, this country room may still be found in use, but only the most old-fashioned houses, loved and lived in by the most old-fashioned kind of people, have a 'butt'ry' these days."

She continues: "The butt'ry (properly spelled *buttery*, of course) is a small room with a smell of good things to eat and a look of delicious plenty. It is located next to the kitchen in the cool corner of the house. . . . Sheathed in warm-colored pine boards, the walls of the butt'ry are lined with hand-planed shelves, sturdy enough to bear the weight of jars, crocks, platters, and plates filled with the richness of country cooking. . . . Every inch of the butt'ry is crowded with goodness."[7]

On his sixth-generation dairy farm that he shares with his wife, Ann, and daughter, Jennifer, Peter Sawyer recalls the pantry, middle pantry, and back pantry that were once a part of their Federal era farmhouse. The original pantry has been incorporated into their present kitchen where there are remnants of cupboards, drawers, and hooks for the large barrels that swung out from below to hold dry staples like flour and sugar. The back pantry was off the woodshed and kept the colder things, while the middle pantry was converted into a bathroom. Meanwhile, Peter's grandparents once had a dumbwaiter with an enclosed cupboard that came up into his grandmother's kitchen from the cold cellar below (it is now anchored underneath the house). For a long time theirs was a three-generation family home and he recalls his grandmother putting on "heavy clothes and going off into the pantry to make bread and work up the dough." As a child he remembers it as "full of stuff and goods and rat holes."

A corner of an early nineteenth-century pantry or butt'ry preserved in a New York farmhouse.

The pantry was not always a nostalgic memory or welcome presence in the farm home. Peter's mother, Elizabeth, was not so fond of the pantry and echoed the sentiments of another contemporary New Hampshire farmwife and writer, Edna Smith Berquist: "In winter the casing cracks let in wind enough to make the pantry icy cold, especially when there was a northeast storm blowing." [In older homes, pantries were usually built on a north corner of a house or ell to take advantage of their cooler location.] The same author recalled her mother's sentiments that "pantries never would have been built into farmhouses if women had any say in the matter," certain they were the creation of men "as torture chambers for their wives." Yet her daughter added, "Mother's pantry always smelled so good. It was a place where we could be pretty sure of finding her . . . we didn't take seriously what Mother said about the pantry."[8]

PANTRIES AND A COMMUNAL KITCHEN

In New Gloucester, Maine, the Sabbathday Shakers—or the United Society of Believers who came to America in 1774 from England—have been living communally for over two hundred years. Their large, brick dwelling house, constructed in 1884, is one of many original structures on the sprawling farm complex of over 1,700 acres. Adjacent to the large kitchen and dining room is a bake room that stores baking supplies and other items for food preparation. Two sliding doors—one in the kitchen and one in the bake room—provided ease of serving and dish clearing from the dining room. Also nearby are two adjoining pantries—one was an ice room lined with shelves for keeping foods cool and the other was a storage pantry with a vent to receive cold air. A cold cellar for vegetables underneath the kitchen utilized the coolness provided by the granite foundation.

Consistent with equality and a strong work ethic, jobs were usually rotated around the communities (Sabbathday Lake is the last remaining active Shaker site). However, women were still largely responsible for the kitchen tasks of bread making, baking, cooking, preserving, and food preparation for the community (at one time several hundred members lived and worked at Sabbathday). As Shakers always embraced the latest technology they incorporated electricity and refrigeration into their kitchen, as well as modern appliances. The simple farmhouse character of the pantries, dining room, and kitchen—all Shaker crafted—remain today and are still used in the private quarters of the four Shakers who continue the faith and the work of their fellowship.

A cold pantry (*right*) once held blocks of ice to cool food. Today it stores all manner of pots and pans and even kerosene lamps, which are often needed in inclement Maine weather. The bake room (*far right*) provides both food storage and additional workspace. A Shaker-made bread table from the 1790s (lower right corner) has a large drawer for rising dough.

FARMHOUSE PANTRY STYLE

❀ COMBINE OPEN WOOD SHELVING WITH DECORATIVE BRACKETS AND CABINETS WITH AUTHENTIC—OR REPRODUCTION—HARDWARE OR WOODEN KNOBS.

❀ WOOD COUNTERS WORK WELL, BUT ALSO CONSIDER MAKING ONE OF MARBLE OR GRANITE FOR ROLLING OUT PIE CRUSTS AND COOKIES.

❀ "MATCHBOARD" WAINSCOTING IS A POPULAR CHOICE FOR WALLS AND CAN BE CARRIED INTO THE KITCHEN AS WELL.

❀ AN OLD ENAMEL OR SOAPSTONE SINK—PERHAPS FROM AN OLD FARMHOUSE—ADDS CHARACTER AND PRACTICAL USE.

❀ HANG OLD LINEN TOWELS ON A VINTAGE TOWEL RACK OR ROLLER AND APRONS FROM HOOKS.

❀ STACK COLORFUL TABLECLOTHS AND OTHER LINENS IN AN UNUSED CORNER OR BASKET.

❀ ARRANGE DISHES AND BOWLS IN RANDOM PILES.

❀ DISPLAY OLD COOKIE CUTTERS IN WOODEN BOWLS AND ANTIQUE KITCHEN ITEMS IN CLUSTERS.

THE
VICTORIAN PANTRY

THE REALM OF DOMESTICITY

Mrs. Isabella Beeton, perhaps the Victorian English equivalent of our Harriet Beecher Stowe, wrote that a good kitchen should have easy access to the scullery, pantry, and storeroom. While estate and farm kitchens spread laterally, the urban kitchen and its associated pantries and workrooms moved vertically, with most operations in dimly lit—and poorly ventilated—cellars. Mrs. Beeton's ideal, with its "excellence of light, height of ceiling, and good ventilation,"[1] could not be utilized by everyone. English cottage kitchens were very much like American farmhouse kitchens, only they had more in common with Early American prototypes.

New and increased technology throughout the nineteenth century led to kitchen changes for the first time in several centuries—cast-iron stoves replaced open fires and the industrial age brought increasing mechanization and tools for the cooking process. Walls were painted or calcimined and floors often had linoleum coverings, another Victorian invention. Water was usually pumped into the kitchen sink. A large worktable could be found in the center of the room. However, unlike its colonial predecessor or contemporary farm kitchen, the Victorian kitchen was typically not a lived-in environment and the urban and suburban kitchen became increasingly industrial.

Most kitchens had pantries for storage and additional workspace. Here were kept sugar and flour barrels while extensive cabinetry—often more than found in the kitchen itself—and open shelving stored all manner of foodstuffs and kitchen implements. Cleaning supplies were also kept here. In more prosperous homes, butler's pantries were serving areas adjacent to the dining room and either above or next to the kitchen.

facing: This unusual screened area of the "big pantry," as it was called, was designed to keep out mice and pests at Woodlands, a Gothic Revival summer home, built in the 1840s in the Georgia mountains.

"All my life, until very recently, I have been opposed to women's suffrage. As I look at it now, I believe it will come before very long—not that I admire that kind of woman. I would have preferred the old scheme, when women did not compete with men, but stayed at home, carried the keys to the pantry and embroidered the samplers of the world. There are a good many men, however, who ought to be embroidering samplers."[2]

—Mr. Emerson Hough, The Woman's Standard, *1911*

A perfectly preserved Victorian pantry and its adjoining kitchen retain their original finish and detail in the cellar of a New England summer home from the turn of the last century.

THE LITERARY PANTRY

Detailed domestic scenes were not uncommon in Victorian period literature. Mary E. Wilkins Freeman (1852–1930) often liked to dwell in the New England farm kitchens and pantries of her novels while Gene Stratton-Porter (1863–1924), a writer from Indiana who described a full and tempting larder in *A Daughter of The Land* (1918), also points to the Victorian concerns of cleanliness and hygiene:

"'I can't come but go to the kitchen—the door is unlocked—you'll find fried chicken and some preserves and pickles in the pantry; the bread box is right there, and the milk and butter are in the spring house.'. . . She was sending him to chicken perfectly cooked, barely cold, melon preserves, pickled cucumbers, and bread like that which had for years taken a County Fair prize each fall; butter yellow as the goldenrod lining the fences, and cream stiff enough to stand alone. Also, he would find neither germ nor mold in her pantry and spring house."[3]

While many authors were writing about the pantry, few may have written *in* the pantry. It is thought that famed nineteenth-century poet Emily Dickinson (1830–86) often wrote poems in her pantry or kitchen, snippets of ideas hastily written onto invoices or receipts. This conveys many things: that Emily also had domestic duties and spent time in the kitchen (we know she used to enjoy making gingerbread for the neighborhood children and lowering it down to them by basket from her bedroom) and that her ideas were fleeting and constant, as so many are. So she scribbled her thin, but sure, lines on any free white space she could find. This implies immediacy—perhaps she had mulled over the words while kneading bread dough or washing dishes and then set out to find something on which to write her poems. A cousin of Emily's, Louise Norcross, said: "I know that Emily Dickinson wrote most emphatic things in the pantry, so cool and quiet, while she skimmed the milk; because I sat on the footstool behind the door, in delight, as she read them to me. The blinds were closed, but through the green slats she saw all those fascinating ups and downs going on outside that she wrote about."[4]

The Victorian kitchen and its workrooms held the domestic pulse of the house, where the comings and goings of the day were most realized, as Emily could observe, even when kitchen quarters and workrooms were in the house or the ell. So she wrote her poems and put them away in her bureau drawer so that perhaps someday someone might find them . . . or not. We credit her sister Lavinia and a household servant with saving these special poetry "preserves," all from the brilliant mind of Emily Dickinson.

This perfectly preserved Victorian kitchen pantry (1858–62) can be seen today as it was left when last in use into the 1980s at the Skolfield-Whittier House, now a museum in Brunswick, Maine.

In urban areas, food was brought to homes via back alleys that ran parallel to the main thoroughfares. Walled-off work yards served as areas for drying linens and accommodated deliveries of food and coal and other provisions for the household. It was also the servants' entrance. In row houses, kitchens were often downstairs and butler's pantries above were equipped with dumbwaiters for efficient transport of food from the kitchen to the pantry where it would be served onto plates or serving dishes.

The rise in technology and new foods cultivated an interest in domestic economy during the Victorian era. Schools in domestic sciences, such as the famed Boston Cooking School and Cornell University, were established to help women with cooking, to train for domestic service, or to assist the farmwife in the newest technology for maximum efficiency. Miss Catharine Beecher and Harriet Beecher Stowe had begun the "kitchen efficiency" mantra in their 1869 publication, *The American Woman's Home,* which advocated, among other things, that everything be in close proximity so as not to repeat too many steps in the kitchen workday.

Women like Maria Parloa (1843–1909), one of the original instructors of the Boston Cooking School, Mary Lincoln (1844–1921), the first principal of the school and editor of its magazine of the same name, and others—especially Fannie Merritt Farmer (1857–1915) and Janet McKenzie Hill (1852–1933)—would define and reshape the American kitchen, and the role of both "housewife" and "domestic," well into the twentieth century. *The Boston Cooking-School Magazine* was founded by Hill in 1896—the same year that Farmer's cookbook came out—and catered exclusively to the housewife. It featured kitchen-tested recipes and articles for the home, including many on how to arrange one's kitchen or pantry. (After 1914 the magazine was known as *American Cookery.*)

"Crusts and pieces of bread should be kept in an earthen pot or pan, closely covered in a cool, dry place.
Keep fresh lard and suet in tin vessels.
Keep salt pork fat in glazed earthenware.
Keep yeast in wood or earthen.
Keep preserves and jellies in glass, china, or stoneware.
Keep salt in a dry place.
Keep meal in a cool, dry place.
Keep ice in the cellar, wrapped in flannel.
Keep vinegar in wood or glass."[5]

—Sarah Josepha Hale,
The Good Housekeeper, 1839

facing, left: This turn-of-the-century butler's pantry in Brooklyn, New York, is typical of late-nineteenth-century urban town houses.

facing, right, top: The butler's pantry at Lyndhurst, a Gothic Revival manor built on the Hudson River, was added in the mid-1860s and features a large and unusually decorative sink and work area directly above the kitchen.

facing, right, bottom: The small but efficient butler's pantry at Gibson House, a preserved Victorian Boston town house built in 1860, came complete with a dumbwaiter and copper-bottomed sink for washing fine china. Servants could communicate to the kitchen below via a speaking tube. This well-appointed home also has several food pantries, a laundry, drying room, and trunk room, all on the ground level adjacent to a coal shed.

IN THE
BUTLER'S
PANTRY

Whether a house had a butler or not, the butler's pantry—or serving pantry—became a distinctive buffer between the kitchen and the dining room. It was a place to serve food and keep it warm, to wash the finest dishes and glassware, and to polish the silver. Symbolically, it was a place between servant and sire. Some butlers in England literally *lived* in their pantry if it was their job to keep the silver and liquor under lock and key.

THE BUTLER DID IT

The butler and his pantry became a popular spot for a "whodunit" in Victorian and twentieth-century fiction. The expression "the butler did it" can likely be traced to novelist Mary Roberts Rinehart (1876–1958), who wrote popular fiction and in 1930 published *The Door*, featuring a criminal butler. In Arthur Conan Doyle's "The Musgrave Ritual," from *The Memoirs of Sherlock Holmes* (1893), the butler Brunton is involved in a crime, and in Agatha Christie's *The Murder of Roger Ackroyd* (1926), Ackroyd's butler Parker, who has "a criminal past," is suspected. The butler was likely an easy mark because of his all-knowing, all-seeing omniscience in the household.

While most writers did not embrace the premise because it was all too obvious, the idea of a tainted butler became an easy target for parody (see also Damon Runyon's 1933 short story "What, No Butler?" and P. G. Wodehouse's 1957 novel *The Butler Did It*).

Meanwhile, the butler sometimes really *did* do it. Perhaps that notion was perpetuated with scandalous front-page events such as in England in 1926 when butler Charles Houghton was charged with murdering his employers, two elderly sisters named Woodhouse. With all the makings of a real potboiler, as another old cliché observes, truth can often be stranger than fiction.[6]

Order in the Butler's Pantry – title page of *Servants' Magazine*, 1 January, 1868

left: The front cover of *The Servants' Magazine*, a publication from Victorian England, depicts a butler polishing silver. The butler was entrusted with lock and key of the family silver and liquor cabinets.

right: Butlers were not always trustworthy, as this article attests. They would also become easy fodder for "whodunits" and English satire.

BUTLER KILLS EMPLOYERS.

Shoots Two Elderly Sisters on English Estate——Taken in Pantry.

Copyright, 1926, by The New York Times Company.
By Wireless to THE NEW YORK TIMES.

LONDON, Sept. 7.—As the result of a sensational shooting affair, Charles Houghton, a butler, was remanded today on a charge of murdering his employers, two elderly sisters named Woodhouse, at their residence, Burghill Court, near Hereford.

It appears that Houghton, who has been employed in the household for over twenty years, was dismissed on Monday and told to leave at once.

Miss Eleanor Woodhouse was passing through the kitchen doorway this morning when a shot was fired and she fell wounded in the throat. Her sister, Martha, hurried to the spot to learn what had happened and was hit by a second shot.

A doctor was called in and found both women dead.

The police had some difficulty in inducing Houghton, who had locked himself in a pantry, to surrender. He was suffering from superficial wounds in his throat, apparently inflicted with a razor.

Women were now encouraged to be in their own kitchens, perhaps assisted by a servant if within their means. "I tell you what, a 'much-traveled woman lecturer' of the period was quoted as saying, 'Nothing gives me the marvelous satisfaction of feeling my own kitchen floor under my two feet,' and she emphasized the remark by bringing one foot and then the other foot down emphatically." [7]

Under the new guise of home economics, the kitchen and its adjacent pantries became a central laboratory for all manner of domestic arts. Except where farm kitchens prevailed, the Victorian kitchen and its turn-of-the-century descendants were studies in efficiency and hygienic methods of cookery and were not intended to be places for dining or gathering. The colonial kitchen and Grandmother's kitchen down on the farm had all but become a pleasant memory.

A primary concern of the home economic movement was kitchen efficiency. This gave rise to smaller kitchens with more useful setups and to space-saving portable cabinetry like the Hoosier and its counterparts. Perhaps the ultimate in economy was when the pantry merged with the kitchen and extended countertops and cabinetry became more prevalent. But in the first few decades of the twentieth century, the kitchen still seemed a Victorian holdover. "I cannot enthuse over the kitchen," said one period writer. "It is all a kitchen should not be . . . so I walk miles in going from pantry to dining room and doing the necessary work." [8]

Others took up the battle cry of efficiency and kitchen reform; some were even prophetic of later-century design, echoing the call of the Beecher sisters in the mid-1800s: "Let us rebel against the kitchen range, which we are persuaded has passed the zenith of its popularity. Let us go even further and abolish the large kitchen entirely. Instead have a room, pantry and kitchen combined, fitted with necessary shelves and cupboards for dishes and cooking utensils." [9]

The Victorian period ended with the struggle for the right to vote, while at the same time there was a crescendo in the home economics movement. It presented a domestic struggle that continues today—can women have it all and have it at the same time? As long as our kitchens are in order—and sinks scoured everyday (as the Beecher sisters preached)—and pantries well stocked, the answer is probably yes. ❧

"Calmness and method . . . are the housekeeper's best friends. Do one thing at a time. (There! I've forgotten my bread in the oven! I put it into bake while I was writing. All burnt on the top! Oh, Dear!) Where was I? Oh, one thing at a time! Don't stop to shed a retrospective tear over old letters in the garret while baking sponge cake, nor hunt for eggs in the barn with the pantry door wide open for the cat to enter in search of a nice dessert. A housekeeper needs her wits about her." [10]

—Mrs. Mary R. P. Hatch, Daughters of America, 1890

This mid-nineteenth-century pantry typifies the kind of kitchen storeroom found in many Victorian homes. A window provided both needed ventilation and light. Note the original graining on the woodwork and matchboard wainscoting.

A KITCHEN PANTRY IN A COUNTRY MANSE

In southern New Hampshire there is a remarkable house that has been in the same family since 1788, evolving very little in time, which has preserved its historical layering. In the mid-1800s an ell (circa 1845–75) was added to the Georgian house and a large period kitchen separated the house from a series of rooms leading to the barn—such as a laundry room, extra bedrooms, and a two-story privy. The woodwork in the kitchen and pantry retains its original graining, and the artist, W. W. H. Greenwood of nearby Peterborough, even signed his handiwork on the inside door under the sink where the inscription remains today (the date is hard to decipher and is in either the 1840s or the 1870s). Graining was a common decorative touch in service areas of Victorian homes where cheaper wood was painted, stained, and combed to look like finer woodwork.

The pantry, in the northeast corner of the room, has an unusual arched wall and retains its original features that include open shelves, a bin for dry goods, cupboards, and drawers. 🌀

left, top: Open shelves built against an unusual curved wall display a variety of kitchen items and foodstuffs, while the floor provides additional areas for food storage where the drafty cold would preserve things longer.

left, bottom: This pantry is full of original nineteenth-century implements, including numerous lidded woodenware pantry boxes and firkins likely made by a local cooper or box factory.

above: The sink, adjacent to the pantry, includes an original drying rack above the work area. On some woodwork below the sink, the grainer signed and dated his handiwork.

left: An old, painted tin box for "Bread & Cake" sits atop a wooden bin for grain or flour.

above: This photograph from the 1890s is remarkable because utilitarian areas of Victorian homes were rarely, if ever, photographed. Inscribed with "Apple Pie," the image was found in a photograph album of the Lambert Bigelow house, "Eastlake," built in 1878 in Shrewsbury, Massachusetts. Not only did a woman, Caroline L. Bigelow, take the picture (she had a darkroom in the home), she likely styled it. A tin cake box, a paper sack, and the makings of apple pie add nostalgic charm to this unusual image.

"One of our prominent divines writes, 'The kitchen decides the health of the household, the fate of sermons, legislative bills and the destiny of empires . . . The kitchen is a workshop, not an exhibition room . . .'"[11]

—Mrs. Mary J. Lincoln, Everyday Housekeeping, 1896

VICTORIAN PANTRY STYLE

In a 1904 article entitled "The Up-to-date Waitress," in the Boston Cooking-School Magazine, the author provided this description of the ideal pantry:

> The pantry (sometimes there are two) is situated between the kitchen and dining room, and opens into each by swinging doors that make no noise; nor are these directly opposite each other. The pantry should be well lighted. The walls of the pantry are lined with enclosed shelves for china and glass, cupboards for the storing of jelly, preserves, pickles, sauces, and cheese designed for immediate use in the dining room. There are also drawers for dish towels, salad cloths, etc. A handsome sink supplied with hot and cold water, and with ample shelf space around it, makes the washing of the tableware a positive pleasure.[12]

- PAINT WOODWORK WHITE OR CREAM OR STAIN WITH A DARK FINISH.

- USE LARGE, STAINED KNOBS OR PERIOD HARDWARE.

- DISPLAY A VARIETY OF CHINA, GLASSWARE, AND OTHER COLLECTIONS IN THE WINDOWED UPPER CABINETS.

- EXTEND CABINETS TO THE CEILING TO MAXIMIZE STORAGE SPACE.

- SET PLATTERS UPRIGHT ON COUNTERTOPS BENEATH CABINETS.

- DISPLAY CANNED GOODS WITH DECORATIVE LABELS AND JARRED PRESERVES TO ADD COLOR.

- USE OLD LIBRARY STAIRS FOR HARD-TO-REACH SHELVES.

- STORE USEFUL MODERN ITEMS IN CUPBOARDS, OUT OF SIGHT, WHILE RESERVING COUNTERTOPS FOR ANTIQUE COLLECTIONS OR EVERYDAY ITEMS.

THE GREAT ESTATE PANTRY

DOMESTIC OFFICES ON A GRAND SCALE

From the end of the nineteenth century until World War I, certain Americans enjoyed an unprecedented boom in wealth and prosperity. In an era when anyone with the right enterprise or invention could make their fortune and become as wealthy as kings, no amount of detail was spared in their homes, even in the servant halls as it required a large and efficient staff to run an estate. Pantries in the great estate homes were numerous and item specific: one might be just for canned goods, another for silver, another for china, and some were even two-storied. Pantries and workrooms were an integral part of an estate kitchen that could prepare dinner for fifty—and another for the household servants—without flinching. These spaces were all about abundance and sumptuousness—storehouses of wealthy accoutrements and foodstuffs.

STAN HYWET HALL

Completed in 1916, Stan Hywet Hall was built in the Tudor Revival style by Goodyear Tire & Rubber Company co-founder Franklin A. Seiberling and his wife, Gertrude Penfield, for their extensive family, in the surrounding countryside of Akron, Ohio. Like other great estates of its day, Stan Hywet was conceived with every amenity and state-of-the art utility, appliance, or thought of comfort for both family and guests. Servants were well provided for with their own quarters, dining room, and other benefits. Those in service would have considered a job at a household of this stature to be a privilege or honor.

This sixty-five-room house had an entire wing devoted to service. On the ground floor was a large and utilitarian commercial-sized kitchen with a butler's pantry that adjoined the dining

facing: A small pantry adjacent to the Stan Hywet breakfast room where the family had most of their meals also served as a kitchenette.

room (including a locked silver vault); a comfortable servant's dining room and various domestic offices for housekeeper, butler, and cook; a food pantry with refrigeration and cupboard space, as well as a place to prepare food; a smaller breakfast room pantry; a flower-arranging room; and a canning storeroom and industrial-sized laundry room in the cellar. On the second and third floors were numerous servant bedrooms, a nursery for visiting children, and many closets and built-in storage cupboards for linens and extra clothing.

above: Housemaids prepare for a large dinner party in this early-twentieth-century print.

facing: Images of a full estate larder at Stan Hywet include canned goods and preserved cherries that await pie making. Cooks preserved all of the fruits and vegetables grown on the estate, especially during World War II.

Echoing the great estates of Britain, no house of this size could function without suitable domestic offices and an efficient staff. The kitchen and its accompanying work and storage rooms were meant to operate like a machine—with the ability to provide lavish, multicoursed dinner parties in the dining room or quieter family meals in the breakfast room on a daily basis.

As expected of women in her position, Mrs. Seiberling was required to oversee the diverse needs of her large household. While a pupil in the 1880s at the Lasell Seminary for Young Women outside of Boston, a young Gertrude took courses in "Domestic Science" and learned about cooking and household management with pioneering instructors and authors such as Maria Parloa, Fannie Farmer, and Mary Lincoln, founder of the Boston Cooking School. Lasell was the first school in the country to offer this emerging discipline and this instruction prepared young women well for all levels of homemaking.

Even though a chatelaine like Mrs. Seiberling was not directly involved in the myriad tasks of her estate, by necessity she had to delegate, manage and run her home like a first-class hotel or much as her husband ran his own company. In addition to the hiring and supervision of a housekeeper or head butler, or both, as well as other staff, Mrs. Seiberling planned detailed weekly menus and consulted daily with the cook about dinner parties, smaller luncheons, afternoon socials, and family gatherings. In its heyday before the 1930s, Stan Hywet Hall employed a head cook, a second cook (who also prepared staff meals), a kitchen maid (who assisted with food preparation), a scullery maid, and waitresses, as needed, for events. The head housekeeper supervised staff and organized the household while the butler primarily oversaw all needs of the table, silver vault, and wine cellar. ✿

SOME NOTES FROM AN ESTATE KITCHEN

In 1944, when this employee ledger was kept by Mrs. Seiberling, the staff at Stan Hywet had diminished to a small handful due to household economy and wartime realities. These kitchen notes are inventory-like and reflect the economy of the times. In addition to its food and butler's pantries, Stan Hywet had a canning room—referred to in notes below as the "fruit cellar"—in the storage areas of the vast cellar and an unusual one fashioned out of a cavelike cistern beneath the Japanese garden.

The extensive grounds of the thirty-year-old estate provided much of the fruit and produce for canning. Mature orchards of peach, apple, plum, and cherry, an extensive grape arbor, and a kitchen garden were available to the kitchen staff. Other fruits and berries were available at local farms or may have grown wild in the 3,000-plus-acre forest that was once part of the estate. Of note is that sugar is often recorded—certainly because of wartime rationing—and menus reflect use of fallen fruit, another frugal gesture.

SUNDAY, JUNE 18:
"Canned 10 qts, 2 pts cherries. Mrs. Perkins' sister came Saturday afternoon remained to help can cherries and stayed until night helping all day to finish cherries picked by Loretta Saturday."

MONDAY, JUNE 27:
"Canned 5 qts. 1 pt white cherries; 16 glasses of jelly: white currants and gooseberries (used 5# sugar)."

SUNDAY, JULY 16:
"Dinner ~ 11 o'clock. Pot roast, potatoes, green beans, fallen peaches, stewed."

MONDAY, JULY 17:
"Tea at 5pm. Apple pie made from fallen apples."

WEDNESDAY, JULY 19:
"Edith and Florence worked cleaning out fruit cellar to prepare for new canned products."

FRIDAY, JULY 28:
"Used 3# sugar. Made 11 glasses blackberry jelly; 4 qts beets canned; 8 jars tomatoes."

MONDAY, AUGUST 14:
"Edith and Florence picked peaches, crabapples and plums. Made 4 pts crabapple butter, 2 pts and 2 glasses plum butter."

THURSDAY & FRIDAY, AUGUST 10 & 11:
"Finished cleaning and stock-taking in store room today (began on August 10)."

FRIDAY, AUGUST 18:
"2 quarts, 1 pt. Peaches & 6 qts of lima beans."

TUESDAY, AUGUST 22:
"Canned 1 large jar of beets and 3 small jars beet relish w/horseradish; 6 quarts blue plums—used a little saccharin for sweetening plums."

FRIDAY, AUGUST 25:
"Peach butter—10 glasses."

THURSDAY, AUGUST 31:
"Canned two quarts and 1 pint red plums for desserts."

FRIDAY, SEPTEMBER 1:
"4 quarts of plums and 3 quarts/1 pint tomato juice." [1]

left, top and bottom: The butler's pantry at Stan Hywet Hall features a pass-through window and two swinging doors that lead into a small corridor buffer between pantry and dining room. The large worktable was where food was plated before serving, usually from the adjacent warming ovens. The room also included a large silver vault.

above: Made of German silver, this butler's pantry sink is one of many at Stan Hywet Hall manufactured by J. L. Mott and was a popular 1910 model.

above: Larger than most period kitchens, this expansive food pantry at Stan Hywet Hall, complete with refrigeration, provided sufficient work space for food preparation as well as storage. Other foodstuffs and preserves were kept in a large canning room in the cellar and in an old cistern on the grounds.

right: The Hoosier cabinet is original to Stan Hywet (c. 1916) and provided a baking center in the corner of the large estate kitchen.

METHODS OF SERVING

Three kinds of table service were used at the multicourse dinner party—Russian, English, and what was called the "Compromise Style." Regardless of which style was used, the large serving pantries at great estates like Stan Hywet were invaluable for assisting in these table operations where food was kept warm and then plated and items were properly stored. These directives are from *The Up-to-date Waitress*, a popular guide to domestic management:

Russian: All food is served " 'from the side' by attendants who pass the food, separated into portions, to the left of those at table, for each to help himself, or made ready on individual plates, it is set down before each individual from the right."

English: "The English style of service breathes hospitality rather than formality. It allows of personal attention, on the part of those sitting at the head and foot of the table, to the needs of those about them." Food is served from the table. The main course "is set down before the 'head of the house' who carves it and selects the portions desired by each." Side dishes are placed on the table as well as bread, butter, and condiments. However, only one course appears at a time on the table.

Compromise: "The compromise style of service, is, as its name implies, a 'let down' from the formality of the Russian service and a 'let up' to the arduous duties expected of the head of the house at an English table." This style was largely used at luncheons and smaller dinner gatherings.[2]

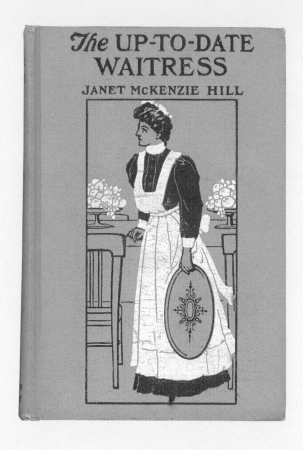

above: This book, written by the founding editor of *The Boston Cooking-School Magazine* (later *American Cookery*), was so popular it came out in several revised editions over the first decades of the twentieth century.

facing: This butler's pantry—constructed between 1920 and 1923 during extensive Colonial Revival–period renovations to a 1791 New England farmhouse—provides a buffer between the dining room and back service ell, as well as stylish storage space not found in a typical farm home.

ESTATE PANTRY STYLE

Great estate pantries were necessary to store the amount of dishes and serving items needed daily and were essentially larger, grander pantries with elements of Victorian design. Some butler's pantries in homes of the grand era were even two-story affairs, complete with up and down storage and access to the upper floor via a ladder or staircase. (The butler's pantry at Biltmore Estate in Asheville, North Carolina, typifies this design.) In some of today's newer and larger homes, butler's pantries and kitchen pantries are returning as popular—and necessary—ancillary kitchen spaces for both storage and entertaining.

above: The well-lit sink area of this 1920s-era butler's pantry adjoins a plant room specifically designed for arranging flowers.

right and facing: This efficient butler's pantry, between the dining room and kitchen of a suburban estate home in the late 1920s, is as large as many contemporary kitchens of its day and is comparable in size to Stan Hywet's butler's pantry: "The serving pantry is 10 x 20 feet. [These dimensions] allow for a worktable—with benches to be shoved underneath when not in use—and also give the necessary floor space. The walls of the pantry above the working counters are sheathed with built-in cupboards; below, by tiers of drawers, except where there are electrical units. There is an abundance of daylight from three tall windows, and powerful ceiling lights illumine the room by night." The owners also installed a large silver closet. [3]

Such essential electrical units *as plate warmer* frigerator, and such equipment as a double sink for dishes for the preparation of salads, make this pantry one of gre A special fireproof silver closet opens from this room i Mrs. George N. Morgan. William P. Whiting, Arc

- ❖ Install a sink for washing dishes in the pantry and use decorative brass or copper fixtures. (Copper-bottomed sinks provided a softer cushion for delicate china.)

- ❖ Have a large worktable in the center of the pantry for sorting dishes or extra space for food preparation.

- ❖ Store silver in felt-lined drawers or custom-made boxes.

- ❖ Place platters in vertical slots underneath counters.

- ❖ Consider a warming oven for ease of food transport.

- ❖ Add an invaluable dumbwaiter if your cellar is also a living space.

- ❖ Store wine or prepared appetizers in under-counter refrigerators to retain the continuity of the countertop.

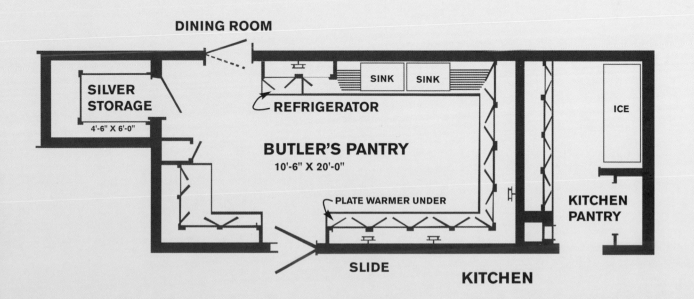

THE
TWENTIETH-
CENTURY PANTRY

ITS RISE, FALL, AND RETURN

During the twentieth century, the pantry enjoyed several decades of continued popularity, yet by the 1950s it had become a thing of the past—something useful and great from Grandmother's era that ended up as a broom closet in a post-war suburban kitchen. The large, open colonial kitchen soon became only a place for nostalgic longing. Food shortages during the world wars—except on farms—helped obliterate the need for food-storage pantries, while a rising middle class that couldn't afford to hire domestic help made the need for a serving pantry almost obsolete. In older homes, pantries were often converted into laundry or utility rooms, breakfast nooks, or other additions to the kitchen.

The pantry as an important workroom continued to be championed until the Second World War, while the mantra of efficiency continued to beat for the housewife. In her concern for kitchen efficiency, Mary Harrod Northend, a historian and writer, acknowledged the needs of the modern woman as a housewife with "outside interests":

> The model housewife gives much consideration to the planning of her kitchen, for the twentieth century woman has so many outside interests that it is necessary for her to prepare her meals in the shortest possible time, eliminating unnecessary steps or motion. In the old-fashioned kitchen of Grandmother's time, she depended on pantry and many closets, wasting much energy, but the housewife of today concentrates her working material close at hand, and as near as may be to the stove.[1]

Meanwhile, there was a growing movement to add decorative interest and charm to the kitchen and its work

facing: This vintage suburban kitchen from the 1950s reflects a whimsical use of color and cabinet design during an era when women were becoming more decorative in their kitchens.

environment. This was a new phenomenon—one that would increasingly take hold as the century moved on. Alice Van Leer Carrick in her popular 1922 book, *The Next-to-Nothing House*, was an early champion of the idea of mixing the practical with personalized décor to create an inviting space in the kitchen and pantry:

> My kitchen today is trim and compact . . . with a good-sized pantry opening from it, two windows (a third in the pantry), five doors and no imagination whatsoever. That quality was my task to supply.
>
> Of course, my color-scheme established at once the decorative truth that I wished to present: a kitchen that should be warm and cheerful, with a sense of simple joys and homely intimacy, rather like a crock of spice cookies or a pan of hot gingerbread. . . . The pantry has

other attractions, too: if your tastes are modern you may admire my porcelain sink, my kitchen cabinet angled discreetly away; if you incline to the antique—there's really no reason why you can't enjoy both; I do.[2]

While the twentieth-century kitchen and its contents were beginning to be more decorative, many pantries were converted into dinettes or breakfast nooks—a 1930s innovation created, perhaps in part, to make the kitchen more lived in. The kitchen was also shrinking in size and often all the space that was afforded, besides in the increased cabinetry, was the broom closet. In the small suburban house, this "catch-all closet" became a place for kitchen pots and pans, brooms, and perhaps a few foodstuffs. One author commented: "One broom closet is all that is usually allotted to a small house, but after figuring the number of steps

Home Baking—the Greatest of all Home Builders

left: The perfect vision of an early-twentieth-century housewife slicing bread.

above: This image from a Star Leaf Lard promotional pamphlet shows an efficient early-twentieth-century kitchen as well as a popular Hoosier cabinet (left).

Make a model pantry with Valspar-Enamel!

This colorful paint ad featured a model twentieth-century pantry. The white painted woodwork and scalloped paper shelf edging were a popular design choice and have been revived in today's pantries.

required to bring the broom from back hall to kitchen for the rest of my life, a kitchen broom closet seemed a necessity."[3]

By the end of World War II, pantries were all but obsolete in American homes, having been absorbed into the cabinetry and countertops of more welcoming and decorative kitchens. Most housewives could get everything they needed at the local market, and more food was being processed, packaged, and made ready to eat. Why have a pantry when you could do your shopping more frequently or make food from a box instead of from scratch? Farmwives still canned and some women still "put up" preserves, but it had become more of a pastime than a need.

With its built-in features in the dining room, the small and ubiquitous bungalow was arguably one of the few original American twentieth-century houses to eliminate the need for a pantry: "The kitchen is well arranged, with the work-table running entirely across one side. It has a California cooler, drawers, flour-bins, spice case, breadboard, cupboard, and all conveniences built in. These built-in furnishings are one of the chief charms of a bungalow and one of the very biggest helps to the modern housekeeper."[4] Other small-scale suburban dwellings simply didn't allow room in their floor plans for a pantry, although there were exceptions. Pantries were in most prewar housing stock and by the 1930s had all but vanished except in larger homes.

The breakfast nook is almost entirely responsible for eradicating the pantry in American homes, while at the same time rescuing the kitchen from domestic oblivion. Once again, as in colonial times, kitchens were becoming more of a

Our Pantry

When we come scooting home from school,
As hungry as a bear,
There's one place that we hustle for,
To see what's waiting there.

And we can always sniff and guess
What mother's left for us;
And then we nibble and explore,
And sometimes make a muss.

Sometimes it's spicy gingerbread,
Or doughnuts, —our surprise;
Sometimes, it's cookies in a jar,
Or little saucer pies.

It's keen, whatever we may find
On mother's pantry shelf.
I hope you have a pantry, or
A cooky jar yourself.

—Daisy D. Stephenson, 1931 (unpublished)

facing: The pass-through pantry at the Riordan House (1904) in Flagstaff, Arizona, reflects the Arts and Crafts built-in styling common around 1900 in bungalows and mansions alike.

THE HOOSIER CABINET— A PANTRY AND KITCHEN IN ONE

The Hoosier—an Indiana invention of the early twentieth century with many imitators—was an outgrowth of the idea of kitchen efficiency and putting everything right at hand for the American housewife (a mid-nineteenth-century idea originally advocated by the Beecher sisters). Period articles, like this one, heralded the design:

"There is today a new kitchen cabinet that few modern housekeepers are able to resist. They come from $13 upwards. They are movable, stand on the floor, and are not as high as the built-in closets. Every bit of space can be utilized. The lower part can be devoted to tin-lined drawers, a very easy matter to arrange for. They can hold flour, bread, cake, and everything that the mice might get at. Even the doors are lined with tin, and when closed it is a neat bit of furniture."[5]

Originally advertised as a pantry replacement, by World War II the Hoosier had grown out of fashion—as had the pantry—replaced by built-in cabinetry and work areas in the kitchen. Today it has become a domestic icon and enduring symbol, popular enough nearly a century later to warrant an entire line of reproductions and replacement parts.

left: This early Hoosier ad reflects the company's appealing marketing strategy of pantry and kitchen work area in one.

facing: The Hoosier cabinet had a variety of built-in features and accessories, including a pull-out work space.

family gathering place. By the late 1920s, housewives were encouraged to "turn an old-fashioned pantry and hallway into a breakfast nook directly off the kitchen or as part of it"[6] but they, too, had their own ideas:

> In a recent house-planning contest of national scope, the judges were unanimous in their report that women had studied the kitchen more carefully than any other parts of the house. They also commented upon the "tremendous demand for built-in features." They found that housewives would abolish the pantry and use the space as a dining alcove, then they would fairly line the kitchen walls with built-in, permanent furniture, the sort that folds up into a wall cabinet being the most popular.[7]

In another article in a 1930 issue of *American Cookery*,

the author describes the emerging kitchen of the mid-twentieth century:

> In the early days of America the kitchen was the center of family life, and a most interesting place it was. . . . In those days the kitchens were large rooms with numerous closets and cupboards. . . . And the kitchen was the most livable room in the whole house. . . . Today almost the opposite situation is apparent. Kitchens are smaller and kitchenettes are popping up everywhere. Fireplaces are never in the kitchen, if they are in the houses at all. We buy in small quantities, we bake in small numbers, and families sometimes live in the fewest of rooms.[8]

One reason that the pantry declined so rapidly after the

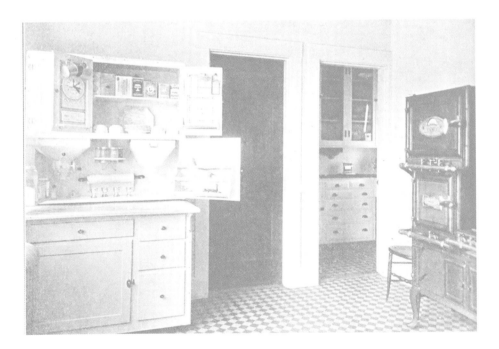

An efficient, laboratory-like kitchen of the early twentieth century would appear to be somewhat of a Victorian holdover if it weren't for the more modern Hoosier cabinet. Note the adjacent pantry—although the Hoosier was marketed as a pantry replacement, in some homes it provided a fitting supplement.

FIRST CHOICE OF
PANTRY RAIDERS

Sure Sign that "BITE SIZE"
Shredded Ralston is their
Favorite Breakfast Cereal

Who can blame these "pantry pi-
rates!" There never was a cereal like
Shredded Ralston! Delicious whole
wheat...ready-to-eat...in a convenient "bite-size" form...with a flavor
that tempts between-meal snacks as
miraculously as it coaxes appetites at
breakfast!

Then don't scold, mother, if boys
and girls find keen delight in eating
Shredded Ralston right out of the
package. It's so nourishing—so easy
to digest—so full of the food-energy
that children need! Keep Shredded
Ralston always in your pantry—for
the youngsters after school—the
whole family every morning!

**Money-back guarantee printed on every
package!** If this delicious whole wheat cereal
doesn't make an instant hit with your family,
the purchase price will be promptly refunded.

IT'S
BITE
SIZE

No Muss...No Crumbling

Shredded
Ralston

The Cereal Millions Eat Because They Like It!

above: The "Pantry Raiders" strike again!

right: An obliging husband seems more than
happy to assist his wife in organizing their
pantry cupboard in this whimsical image from
the *New York Times* in 1944.

A Bride's Pantry

There's a dear little pantry that pampers a bride,
Its walls are of yellow, its window is wide,
And airy blue curtains coquette in their pride
With crisp, crinkled things in the garden outside.

There are quaint little jars with blue labels displayed,
For red currant jelly and plum marmalade;
There are vegetable soldiers in tin coat parade,
Plump jugs of sweet cider and muscadine-ade.

Oh, the goodies galore that a bride can devise—
Fat gingerbread bunnies with black raisin eyes,
Spice cake and pear salad and cinnamon pies,
To foster the pride in a certain man's eyes.

So when you are planning a little house, new,
Be sure there's a pantry with curtains of blue,
And a wee kitchen garden spread out to your view,
To grow with your singing and smile back at you.[9]

—Hazel Harper Harris, American Cookery, 1925

Big 6-page "Festive Food" Feature

Here's Our
Cupboard-Full
of
Special
"TREATS"

All happily yours,
from pantry-to-table
in minutes!

Betty Crocker
Pantry Jubilee

Remember the grand old-fashioned foods that used to take hours
to prepare? Today's modern food ideas are just as delicious
and so much faster! CLIP AND SAVE the 14 wonderfully easy
new "recipe-ideas" on the following pages!

An early version of Betty Crocker greets magazine readers from her pantry cupboard. Note the knotty-pine door and old-style door latch—stylistic elements of the Early American revival that predominated in the 1950s. The ad says: "Remember the grand old-fashioned foods that used to take hours to prepare?" The idea was to preserve the nostalgia of Grandmother's pantry while making things effortless in the kitchen.

Second World War was that not only had the size of American housing shrunk significantly but that wartime rationing and concerns about hoarding made extended food storage unthinkable. (Kitchens were an average of eighty square feet versus several hundred feet in the early twenty-first century.) A postwar article on the latest gourmet products for the pantry in late 1946 was both breezy and enthusiastic: "Any mention of stocking the pantry was frowned upon during the war, smacking as it did of hoarding, but now that things are more nearly normal, at least in grocery circles, it once again becomes a pleasant duty of the fall season to stow away a few products on a closet shelf, especially for partying purposes."[10]

The cold war brought about another kind of pantry in American homes: the atomic bomb shelter. Because of the threat of another world war, the Federal Civil Defense Administration's "Operation Cue" asked Americans to establish short-term pantries, despite what seems like a naïve posture: "The 7-day pantry [we] ask you to set up has a grimmer, and more urgent, purpose than Grandma's 'Emergency Shelf'—it can save your family's lives in case of atomic attack."[11]

By the 1950s and '60s, apart from any stockpiling that occurred in the atomic age, pantries could only be found in older homes from Grandmother's era and had often languished into utility or laundry rooms. Postwar houses were small and efficient and didn't have room for a pantry—instead they were lucky to have a broom closet. In a 1964 magazine article, the idea was to "bring the pantry back to the kitchen" by adding lots of "adequate and convenient storage space," which included floor-to-ceiling closets within the kitchen.

THE CHILDREN'S PANTRY

During the first few decades of the twentieth century, the pantry became a favorite spot for childhood antics and storylines in numerous children's books and literature. In Johnny Gruelle's beloved *Raggedy Anne Stories* (1918), Anne leads the other dolls in a messy pantry raid (a prevalent theme in period children's stories). The works of Lucy M. Montgomery in the *Anne of Green Gables* series provide many descriptions of pantry comings and goings and a domestic picture of the day. Meanwhile, in *These Happy Golden Years,* Laura Ingalls Wilder wrote a several-page narrative description of the pantry that Almanzo built for her in 1885 in their first home together in DeSmet, South Dakota. It describes, in wonderful detail, an elaborate farmhouse pantry in which she obviously delighted and took great pride.

In the tales of English illustrator Beatrix Potter, many of her animals get into mischief in their various larders, pantries, and cupboards. In Kenneth Grahame's *The Wind in the Willows,* Toad, Rat, Mole, and Badger take back Toad Hall from the weasels and stoats via a secret trap door in the butler's pantry. Perhaps the most famous literary example of a pantry-related incident was when Mark Twain's Tom Sawyer did penance for his raid on Aunt Polly's jam by having to whitewash her picket fence.

left: Pantry raiding was a popular pastime among children and is often described in children's literature and nostalgic poetry from the era.

above: The cozy and cute nature of a pantry often provided the perfect setting for a children's story or a backdrop to a kitchen-related event.

This would become a prevalent notion in built-in cabinetry in the second half of the twentieth century. [12] Butlers and their pantries still existed, of course, but usually only in the largest or wealthiest of homes. During the extensive White House restorations of the early 1960s, for example, President and Mrs. Kennedy saw the need for a butler's pantry in their own quarters. Two years later, it was front-page news when President Kennedy cut his finger slicing bread in that pantry.

Unlike the sterile Victorian workrooms and their even smaller successors, today's kitchen—whether large or small—is the deliberate center of the American home. Today there is a return to building large new houses and "estate" homes or restoring historic housing stock, often with old pantries and storerooms still present. According to a 2005 National Association of Home Builders survey, walk-in pantries are the most requested feature in kitchens today. [13] Perhaps it is the popular return of home cooking and baking. Perhaps it stems from the 1990s trend of nesting and stockpiling for the "new millennium," world disaster, or a cozy blizzard. Perhaps it is because a good pantry makes sense.

In 1932, when small kitchens began to be the norm well before World War II, *American Cookery* magazine recalled the kitchens of the past: "Where now is cider drunk and apples eaten? Where is the Virginia reel danced? Where is there every evening the laughter and joy of friends and family, the telling of good stories, the propounding of conundrums? Perhaps old families have shrunk as has the old-time kitchen. . . . So much for the great, roomy, old-time kitchen, that was dining room, living room, workroom and playroom, the kitchen of the past." They also had a prophetic request for the kitchens and open-concept households of the future, which would again embrace the kitchens of their colonial ancestors: "We hope the swing of the pendulum will make it right for home-building architects to frame a scheme where the whole ground floor of the house shall be one large, hospitable kitchen, to cook in and eat in and work in and play in, and live happily in ever after." [14]

"With their home transformed into a police centre and every room on the ground floor occupied, Colonel and Mrs. Lindbergh slipped away together for a few minutes tonight from the turmoil and enjoyed a pantry lunch in the small alcove off the kitchen of their home. . . . The young mother came downstairs tonight and beckoned to her husband. Together they went to the pantry and the Colonel engaged in the homely task of buttering bread for sandwiches while Mrs. Lindbergh removed the cap from a milk bottle and poured its contents into two glasses." [15]

—The New York Times, *March 7, 1932*

THE WARTIME PANTRY

During the two world wars, despite the increased availability of canned goods, American women were called upon to put up their own food. By this time, hot pack canning was considered the most reliable and, with "two hours from garden to can," the rule to follow. A 1942 article detailed the effort:

> This year, American homemakers are canning at home as a patriotic duty, for it is especially important that no food be allowed to go to waste during the summer and fall. . . . From the standpoints of family health and economy, the canning of vegetables from Victory Gardens, and homegrown or locally gathered wild fruits, and also reasonably priced fresh products on the market is one of the homemaker's important contributions to the wartime nutrition program.

Because sugar was an essential canning ingredient, home canners were also allowed special privileges: "According to regulations issued by the OPA, effective May 19, 1942, each home canner will be permitted to purchase 'an amount not to exceed one pound of sugar for canning each four quarts of finished fruit.' Finished fruit means that which is prepared, heated and ready to be packed with jars, or actually four quarts of canned fruit."[16]

This pamphlet was among many distributed during the atomic age to promote a stockpiling of supplies in the event of catastrophe. Members of the Mormon church are still advised to keep a year's supply of food in the event of disaster.

A PAIR OF TURN-OF-THE-CENTURY PANTRIES PROVIDE VINTAGE CHARM

A Michigan-raised professional baker and cook, who for a time worked in several Boston cafés, shares an 1890 shingle-style house with her husband. She has loved pantries since she was a young girl, and their home is fortunate to have two original intact pantries with shelves, drawers, cupboards, and hardware—all part of the architect's original plan found in the attic of their house. One pantry—called a "china closet" on the plan—connects the dining room with the kitchen; the other is an adjacent storage pantry opening into the kitchen. Both have windows with southern exposure and are approximately 6 x 6 feet. There is even room for a beloved period Hoosier along the wall space between the pantry doors. These pantries reflect period sensibility and continue as practical, efficient, and attractive work spaces. The owners couldn't be happier in their restored kitchen and its workrooms. ❧

above: A view of the two original pantries in this 1890 home. The kitchen was recently restored to the period, but the pantries only needed a new coat of paint.

facing: This kitchen pantry from 1890 is small but efficient and retains all of its original features, such as authentic hardware and recessed paneling on cabinets, which are widely copied in today's homes.

"Men talk about women's sphere being in the home and then assume that she is satisfied if the pantry is well filled and the rooms warmed."[17]

—"Home Notes,"
The Woman's Standard,
1894

facing: The "china closet," so noted on the house's original plan, has a sliding window-like door and serves as a walk-through from kitchen to dining room. Its window, baking shelf, and white enamel finish all typify the description of an ideal pantry (right).

TWENTIETH-CENTURY PANTRY STYLE

While gradually becoming more streamlined, the pantry continued to be fashioned using tenets of Victorian style. An article in 1908 on "A Practical Kitchen" in the Boston Cooking-School Magazine *sums up the features of pantries continuing to be built in American homes into the twentieth century:*

The very keynote of the up-to-date home is the saving of steps, the elimination of unnecessary labor, and the lightening in every possible way of work that is necessary . . . The arrangement of the pantry, with its stores and utensils, if done with care, will save much time and labor. The pantry should be very near the sink and table, and there should be a broad shelf on which much of the baking may be prepared. Every pantry should have a window, both for light and ventilation, and if shelves and woodwork are finished in white enamel, there is no need for covers of oil-cloth or paper.[18]

THE MODERN PANTRY

WHERE EVERYTHING OLD IS NEW AGAIN

The term *modern pantry* is somewhat of an oxymoron. So many of the pantries in today's homes, while new in construction, are vintage in feel. Others are sleek and modern reinterpretations. Despite their style, pantries of today share much in common with their ancestors in their ample and diverse storage space. In the twenty-first century, the pantry has gained great popularity in new homes, and some historic home owners are even reconverting pantry spaces that languished into mudrooms, bathrooms, or storage closets back to their original form and purpose.

Our kitchens are no longer relegated to a back corner of the house. They are full-blown theatrical showplaces with the latest state-of-the-art appliances or, once again, the cozy kitchen-living-work areas of another era long ago. The tiny antisocial confines of a utilitarian Victorian kitchen or a small suburban kitchen away from the social life and the parties have emerged into a kitchen that is again central to the home, as in the colonial period. Naturally, in our demand for a larger kitchen we also want a pantry again—if not for food storage or utensil overflow, then at least as a nod to the practical and attractive storage of the past. A popular concept of today is the "farmhouse kitchen," which, in its prevalent use of matchboard and open shelves with decorative brackets, has brought Grandmother's pantry right *into* it.

A funny thing happened on the way to the millennium: we began to cook more, bake more, buy more, and stockpile more. We not only enjoy power shopping at large wholesale grocery stores, but we like to have something on hand for a rainy day or

facing: This modern pantry in Manhattan is renovated from the early twentieth century when butler's pantries were prevalent features in urban apartments.

a possible catastrophe. Having ample supplies at the ready is a secure assurance of the progressing pace of the modern world—and having a full pantry is about provision for ourselves and our loved ones, about staving off the world at large while we maintain a semblance of order and security in our own kitchens.

Ironically, the pantry is again popular despite that most twenty-first-century kitchens have more countertops and cabinets than those in any other era of our domestic past.

Near our large kitchens, we also want that cozy, well-ordered room where we might be reminded of our grandmother's house or where we know that somehow in a crazy world, a full larder will keep us safe—or at least well supplied in canned goods and other delights.

Pantries don't have to be all about foodstuffs either—dishes and collections are just as "at home" in a cupboard or closet. This chapter provides further design inspirations for pantries new or old—and ways to display your collections. ✿

IDEAS FOR CREATING
YOUR OWN PANTRY

This butler's pantry was installed in 2001 in an 1813 Federal house. Its matching twin pantry is adjacent to it, and it is likely that the original pantries were at this location. Built for an extensive collection of dishes, glassware, and silver, the pantry features glass cabinets that extend to the ceiling and ample cupboard storage below. Drawers provide room for linens, while the cupboards hold larger items and vertical spacing for trays and platters. The countertop was constructed with recycled mahogany from another project, which is cheaper than many other woods and extremely durable. Ideally, if used for food storage or preparation, pantries should have windows for ventilation—as this room did before the new kitchen ell was added in 1816—however, butler's pantries were often interior rooms. The hardware and white cream paint treatment

recalls a pantry from the 1890s or later and is a popular look in today's homes.

Pantries can be built in small spaces, large closets, or even larger rooms. It is important to allow counter space for preparing food or placing dishes for use. Pantries are ideal for narrower spaces, because not much room is needed between cabinets unless you want space for a table or work island. It is not necessary to hire an architect; all you need is a good cabinetmaker. Here the owners gave the carpenters their design for a cupboard support bracket, which they had sketched, and showed them photos from magazines for design inspiration. The cabinetry was completed in several weeks, and in an additional week the pantry was painted and wallpapered. If a more modern look is desired, premade built-ins can also be purchased from a variety of department stores and companies.

facing: This butler's pantry is one of two modern Victorian-style pantries constructed in a Federal period home. Reproduction hardware is used for latches and drawer pulls.

AN INVENTIVE PANTRY AND ADAPTED HOOSIER ADD SPACE AND COLOR

In 1995, Judy Johnson decided she needed more storage space, so she started tearing out chunks of drywall between two wall studs around the corner from her small and tidy galley kitchen. Her Cape-style home, built by her husband, Charlie, in 1973, is efficient and practical out of necessity. Within a few hours sufficient space was cleared to store jars of herbs and spices and tins of tea and other small staples. Charlie added shelves and finished the pantry-in-the-wall with two painted shutters that serve as decorative doors in the cottage tradition. Now Judy couldn't be happier with her whimsical approach to "found" storage and says it is the best project she and her husband have ever done.

Meanwhile, in the nearby dining area of this tiny but attractive house, Judy took an old Hoosier-style cabinet, removed its cupboard doors, painted it white, and filled it with her extensive collection of LuRay pastels that started years ago with a handful of dishes from her grandmother. Now a decorative and colorful china pantry—while useful—it is also a perfect place to display a collection. Both of Judy's innovations are creative features that prove anyone can have a pantry if they so desire, despite the limitations of a floor plan. ✿

"*Organizing the household was another matter entirely. There was something fulfilling about that, something consoling—or more than consoling; it gave him the sense of warding off a danger. Over the next week or so, he traveled through the rooms setting up new systems. He radically rearranged all the kitchen cupboards, tossing out the little bits of things in sticky, dusty bottles.*"[1]

—Anne Tyler, The Accidental Tourist

A ready pantry is created between the wall studs and behind an old shutter for a door.

An old Hoosier-style cabinet is revamped for use as a
display cabinet for a beloved collection of LuRay.

MODERN PANTRY STYLE

Pantries of today are recollections of earlier pantries or are equally practical spaces that use modern materials like chrome and specialty woods. The pantry hasn't changed much over its several-hundred-year history except in the use of materials. Most pantries are small rooms with shelves and cupboards and are recognizable as such. Your own collections and preferences will help inspire the era or design of your pantry. Here are some design features that would be welcome in any pantry:

* OPEN SHELVING, OFTEN WITH WOODEN BRACKETS OR HARDWARE

* PAINTED OR STAINED SURFACES FOR A VINTAGE LOOK

* CHROME OR STAINLESS STEEL FOR A MODERN LOOK

* COMPLEMENTARY HARDWARE (WHETHER REPRODUCTION, HISTORIC, OR MODERN, THE HARDWARE SHOULD BE PRACTICAL AND NOT OVERWHELM THE LOOK OF YOUR PANTRY.)

* CUPBOARDS BELOW COUNTERTOPS FOR STORING LARGE ITEMS

* VERTICAL OR HORIZONTAL SLOTS FOR PLATTERS AND LARGE ITEMS

* DIVIDED DRAWERS FOR LINENS OR SILVERWARE

* SCALLOPED SHELF PAPER (ATTACH TO THE EDGES OF CUPBOARDS OR SHELVES FOR A TRADITIONAL LOOK. THIS IS A FUSSY BUT ATTRACTIVE HOLDOVER FROM THE VICTORIAN PERIOD.)

* VINTAGE COLLECTIONS, OLD LABELS, OR DECALS ON PANTRY ITEMS, SUCH AS JARS, TINS, AND CANISTERS

facing: In the renovation of their kitchen and pantry, the owners of this 1926 home were inspired by a vintage rooster kitchen motif.

WHAT TO PUT
IN YOUR PANTRY

Pantries can be devoted exclusively to food, china, or antique collections or may include a combination of everything (as in the facing pantry). Here are some ideas to inspire your own pantry creations:

❁ HIDDEN BINS FOR STAPLES LIKE FLOUR, RICE, OR DOG FOOD

❁ BASKETS OR METAL BINS FOR FOOD STORAGE

❁ LARGE VINTAGE OR MODERN TINS AND CANISTERS

❁ GLASS JARS FOR FOODSTUFFS LIKE DRIED PEAS, PASTA, BEANS, CHOCOLATE CHIPS, ETC.

❁ SPICE JARS AND CANISTERS WITH OLD OR NEW LABELS

❁ CANNED GOODS AND GOURMET FOODSTUFFS

❁ DISHES COMBINED WITH FOOD STORAGE

❁ EVERYDAY DISHES OR ANTIQUE COLLECTIONS

❁ COOKBOOKS—WELL-LOVED FAVORITES OR YOUR GRANDMOTHER'S SPECIAL HEIRLOOMS

❁ ANTIQUE LINENS OR PILES OF COLORFUL ASSORTED DISH TOWELS AND TABLECLOTHS

❁ SHAKER PEGS OR CAST-IRON HOOKS FOR YOUR VINTAGE APRONS (EVEN IF YOU NEVER WEAR THEM, THEY LOOK GREAT HANGING UP!)

above, left: A Roylace ad for scalloped shelf paper appealed to pantry owners.

above, right: A Potting Pantry: An old, worn cupboard makes an ideal location for a pantry to store and display garden items. This one is in the shed of an old barn but would easily work inside the house, too.

facing: A Linen Pantry: Pantries can be devoted exclusively to linens, such as in this old Italianate house in Upstate New York.

ENDNOTES

IN THE PANTRY
[1] Lydia Lion Roberts, "Remembered Rooms," *American Cookery* 30, no.1 (June–July 1925): 5.
[2] Beatrice Wilson, "The Book on the Pantry Shelf," *Farm Journal and Farmer's Wife* (February 1945): 74.

EARLY AMERICAN PANTRY
[1] Edna Knowles King, "That Very Important Room, the Kitchen," *American Cookery* 35, no.6 (January 1931): 426.
[2] Stuart Bartlett, "The Great 'Lazy Susan'," *Old-Time New England* 36, no. 1 (July 1945): 8–11.
[3] "The Washingtons at Home," *Journal of Home Economics* 24, no. 2, (February 1932): 142–145.
[4] Alice Morse Earle, *Home Life in Colonial Days* (New York: The Macmillan Company, 1926), 52.

FARMHOUSE PANTRY
[1] Harriet Beecher Stowe, "Preparing for a Tea Party in 17—," in *The Minister's Wooing*. (Boston: Houghton Mifflin Co., 1896).
[2] Della T. Lutes, *Home Grown* (Boston: Little, Brown and Company, 1937), 235.
[3] Haydn S. Pearson, *New England Flavor: Memories of a Country Boyhood* (New York: W.W. Norton & Company, Inc., 1961), 135–37.
[4] Marjorie Kinnan Rawlings, *Cross Creek Cookery* (New York: Charles Scribner's Sons, 1942), 183.
[5] Annie Curd, "Fruit Jellies," *The Home-Maker* 4, no. 5 (August 1890): 408–9.
[6] A. B. Braley, "My Mother's Cooky Jar," *The Boston Cooking-School Magazine* (later *American Cookery*) XI, no. 2 (August–September 1906): 99.
[7] Mary Mason Campbell, *The New England Butt'ry Shelf Cookbook*. Brattleboro: Stephen Greene Press, 1982; originally published in 1968 by the World Publishing Company.
[8] Edna Smith Berquist, *The High Maples Farm Cookbook* (New York: Macmillan Company, 1971), 116–17.

VICTORIAN PANTRY
[1] Mrs. Isabella Beeton, *Mrs. Beeton's Book of Household Management* (Oxford: Oxford University Press, 2000), 39.
[2] Mr. Emerson Hough, "Change of Mind," *The Woman's Standard* 23, no. 10 (February 1911): 4.
[3] Gene Stratton-Porter, *A Daughter of the Land,* (New York: Doubleday, Page & Company, 1918), 459–60.
[4] Gary Scharnhorst, "A Glimpse of Dickinson at Work," *American Literature* 57.3 (1985): 483–85.

[5] Sarah Josepha Hale, *The Good Housekeeper* (Boston: Weeks, Joran & Company, 1839).
[6] Cecil Adams, "In whodunits, it's 'the butler did it.' Who did it first?," The Straight Dope, http://www.straightdope.com/columns/030926.html (accessed April 15, 2006).
[7] Emma Gary Wallace, "Come On Out Into the Kitchen," *American Cookery* 40, no. 1 (June–July 1935): 20–24.
[8] Editorial, "Home Making For One," *Everyday Housekeeping (The American Kitchen Magazine 1895–1903)* 7, no. 4 (July 1897): 129–31.
[9] Angie Tower Curtis, "How to Save Strength and Time," *Everyday Housekeeping (The American Kitchen Magazine 1895–1903)* 5, no. 5, August 1896, 26–27.
[10] Mrs. Mary R. P. Hatch, "Preaching and Practicing," *Daughters of America* 4, no. 3 (March 1890): 6.
[11] Mrs. Mary J. Lincoln, "Furnishing a Model Home," *Everyday Housekeeping (The American Kitchen Magazine 1895–1903)* 5, no. 6 (September 1896): 68–71.
[12] "The Up-to-date Waitress," (Third Paper), *The Boston Cooking-School Magazine* (later *American Cookery*) 9, no. 3 (October 1904): 160–62.

GREAT ESTATE PANTRY
[1] "Employee Ledger," Gertrude Penfield Seiberling, 1944, Stan Hywet Hall & Gardens, Akron, Ohio.
[2] "The Up-to-date Waitress," *The Boston Cooking-School Magazine* (later *American Cookery*) 9, no. 3 (October 1904): 160–62.
[3] Harriet Sisson Gillespie, "The Function of the Serving Pantry: A Vital Link in the Chain of Domestic Machinery," *The House Beautiful* 66, no. 3 (September 1929): 295.

TWENTIETH-CENTURY PANTRY
[1] Mary Harrod Northend, "The Sanitary Kitchen," *The Modern Priscilla* 33, no. 8 (October 1919): 53.
[2] Alice Van Leer Carrick, *The Next-to-Nothing House* (Boston: The Atlantic Monthly Press, 1922) 111–25.
[3] Jane Scott, "Corners of the New House," *American Cookery* 39, no. 5 (December 1934): 282–84.
[4] E. Lundborg, Architect, "Ye Bungalow," *The Modern Priscilla* 28 (May 1914): 52.
[5] E. M. H., "The Up-to-Date Kitchen," *American Cookery* 20, no. 6 (January 1916): 429.
[6] Lester G. Herbert, "Some Refinements You Can Add to Your Home," *American Cookery* 33, no. 8 (March 1929): 604–5.
[7] Bertha Streeter, "Other Women's Kitchen Conveniences," *American Cookery* 31, no. 7 (February 1927): 509.
[8] M. Louise C. Hastings, "How Does Your Kitchen Look?" *American Cookery* 34, no. 7 (February 1930): 542.

[9] Hazel Harper Harris, "A Bride's Pantry," *American Cookery* 29, no. 8 (March 1925): 610.

[10] Jane Nickerson, "For the Pantry," *The New York Times*, September 8, 1946.

[11] Editorial, "Grandma's Pantry NEW STYLE," *The American Home* 58, no. 5 (September 1955): 70.

[12] Virginia T. Habeeb, "The Pantry-Shelf Kitchen: A Fresh Look at Kitchen Design," *The American Home* 67, no. 1 (January–February 1964): 80–82.

[13] National Association of Home Builders, "Latest Housing Consumer Trends Focus on Upscale Amenities, http://www.nahb.org/news_details.aspx?newsID=1483.

[14] Editorial, "Old-Time Kitchens and New," *American Cookery* 37, no. 5 (December 1932): 343.

[15] "Lindbergh and Wife Meet in Pantry for Night Lunch," *The New York Times*, March 7, 1932, 1.

[16] Doris W. McCray, "The Hot Pack Method Makes Wartime Canning Simple, Safe and Sure," *American Cookery* 47, no. 2 (August–September 1942): 46–47.

[17] Editorial, "Home Notes," *The Woman's Standard* 8, no. 6 (February 1894): 6.

[18] Fleeta Wheeler, "A Practical Kitchen," *The Boston Cooking-School Magazine* (later *American Cookery*) 13, no. 4 (November 1908): 179–80.

MODERN PANTRY
[1] Anne Tyler, *The Accidental Tourist* (New York: Knopf, 1985), 42.

LAST PAGE
[1] Eugene Field, *The House* (New York: Charles Scribner's Sons, 1896), 226.

SOURCES FOR THE PANTRY

The following list offers some places to acquire pantry-related storage items (new or vintage) or services. Antique shops and flea markets—as well as eBay—are great places to find pantry-related antiques like storage jars, canisters, and all manner of utensils.

ANTHROPOLOGIE
Anthropologie.com

CALIFORNIA CLOSETS
CaliforniaClosets.com

CRACKER BARREL
Old Country Store and
Restaurant(s)
CrackerBarrel.com

CRATE & BARREL
CrateandBarrel.com

CROWN POINT CABINETRY
Crown-Point.com

EBAY
eBay.com

GOOSEBERRY PATCH
GooseberryPatch.com

IKEA
IKEA.com

I.U. TRIPP & CO.
IUTripp.com

KENNEDY HARDWARE
KennedyHardware.com

KING ARTHUR FLOUR
KingArthurFlour.com

LEHMAN'S
Lehmans.com

RESTORATION HARDWARE
RestorationHardware.com

STONEWALL KITCHEN
StonewallKitchen.com

TARGET
Target.com

VERMONT COUNTRY STORE
VermontCountryStore.com

VINTAGE KITCHENS
VintageKitchens.com

WILLIAMS-SONOMA
Williams-Sonoma.com

PANTRIES OPEN TO THE PUBLIC

*FEATURED IN *The Pantry*

Most historic house museums now include a building's domestic workings—or "offices" like the pantry and other related kitchen spaces—in their tours. The following organizations or individual properties are open at different times throughout the year—please check in advance—and are but a sampling of house museums throughout the United States:

*BILTMORE ESTATE
1 Approach Road
Asheville, NC 28803
800-624-1575
Biltmore.com

BOSCOBEL RESTORATION, INC.
1601 Route 9D
Garrison, NY 10524
845-265-3638
Boscobel.org

*CONSTABLE HALL
PO Box 36, John Street
Constableville, NY 13325
315-397-2323
ConstableHall.org

*EMILY DICKINSON MUSEUM
The Homestead & The Evergreens
280 Main Street
Amherst, MA 01002
413-542-8161
EmilyDickinsonMuseum.org

GAMBLE HOUSE
4 Westmoreland Place
Pasadena, CA 91103
626-793-3334
GambleHouse.org

*GIBSON HOUSE MUSEUM
137 Beacon Street
Boston, MA 02116
617-267-6338
TheGibsonHouse.org

HARRIET BEECHER STOWE
HOUSE & LIBRARY
77 Forest Street
Hartford, CT 06105
860-522-9258
HarrietBeecherStowe.org

*HISTORIC NEW ENGLAND, INC.
141 Cambridge Street
Boston, MA 02114
617-227-3956
HistoricNewEngland.org

*LYNDHURST
National Trust for Historic
Preservation
635 South Broadway
Tarrytown, NY 10591
914-631-4481
Lyndhurst.org or
NationalTrust.org

*MARJORIE KINNAN RAWLINGS
HISTORIC STATE PARK
18700 South County Road 325
Cross Creek, FL 32640
352-466-3672
FloridaStateParks.org

MUHEIM HERITAGE HOUSE
207 Youngblood Hill
PO Box 14
Bisbee, AZ 85603
520-432-7698
BisbeeMuseum.org

*OLD STURBRIDGE VILLAGE (OSV)
1 Old Sturbridge Village Road
Sturbridge, MA 01566
800-SEE-1830
OSV.org

PRESERVATION SOCIETY OF
NEWPORT COUNTY
424 Bellevue Avenue
Newport, RI 02840
401-847-1000
NewportMansions.org

*RIORDAN MANSION
State Historic Park
409 West Riordan Road
Flagstaff, AZ 86001
928-779-4395
pr.state.az.us

*SABBATHDAY LAKE SHAKER
MUSEUM
The United Society of Shakers
707 Shaker Road
New Gloucester, ME 04260
207-926-4597
shaker.lib.me.us/museum.html

NOTE: *Pantries are located in the private Shaker dwelling house and are not open to the general public. However, other buildings are open during regular hours of operation by guided tour.*

*SKOLFIELD-WHITTIER HOUSE
MUSEUM
Pejepscot Historical Society
159-161 Park Row
Brunswick, ME 04011
207-729-6606
CurtisLibrary.com/Pejepscot.htm

*STAN HYWET HALL & GARDENS
714 North Portage Path
Akron, OH 44303
888-836-5533
StanHywet.org

*THERON BOYD HOUSE
(access by permission)
Vermont Division for
Historic Preservation
National Life Building—Drawer 20
Montpelier, VT 05620
802-828-3211
HistoricVermont.org

*YODER'S AMISH HOME
6050 State Route 515
Millersburg, OH 44654
330-893-2541
YodersAmishHome.com

*ZADOCK PRATT MUSEUM
PO Box 333, Main Street
Prattsville, NY 12468
518-299-3395
PrattMuseum.com

PHOTO CREDITS AND PERMISSIONS

❀

All photographs © Susan Daley and Steve Gross (212-679-4606) except for the following:

Photographs on pages 18, 33, & 38 © Catherine Seiberling Pond

Photographs on pages 52 & 55–57 © Daniel Milner for Stan Hywet Hall & Gardens

Cover photograph © F & E Schmidt Photography

Image on page 16 © 1964 Old Sturbridge Village. Reprinted by permission. From a pamphlet written by Abbott Lowell Cummings, *Architecture in Early New England*. Old Sturbridge Village, Sturbridge, Massachusetts, 1964.

Image on page 21 © 1945 Historic New England, Boston, Massachusetts. Reprinted by permission. Stuart Bartlett, "The Great 'Lazy Susan'," *Old-Time New England* 36, no. 1 (July 1945): 8–11.

Image on page 46 (right) © 1926 The New York Times Co. Reprinted by permission. "Butler Kills Employers—Shoots Two Elderly Sisters on English Estate—Taken in Pantry," *The New York Times*, September 8, 1926, 2.

Image on page 50 © John M. Carpenter. Reprinted by permission.

Image on page 71 (right) © 1944 The New York Times Co. Reprinted by permission. Jane Holt, "Stocking the Pantry," *The New York Times*, October 8, 1944, 104.

Endnote 10 on page 72 © 1946 The New York Times Co. Reprinted by permission.

Endnote 15 on page 74 © 1932 The New York Times Co. Reprinted by permission.

Endnote 1 on page 84 © 1985 *The Accidental Tourist* by Anne Tyler. Knopf is now a division of Random House, Inc. Reprinted by permission.

Most of the archival images and footnoted sources used in this book are within the public domain. If not, every attempt was made to contact rightful copyright owners. The author apologizes for any error or oversight.

The author would like to thank the following online and actual archives and collections for their invaluable resources:

FEEDING AMERICA: The Historic American Cookbook Project. East Lansing, MI: Michigan State University Library & Museum. http://digital.lib.msu.edu/projects/cookbooks/index.html (2005)

HOME ECONOMICS ARCHIVE: Research, Tradition and History (HEARTH). Ithaca, NY: Albert R. Mann Library, Cornell University. http://hearth.library.cornell.edu (2006)

INTERNATIONAL WOMEN'S PERIODICALS: Ithaca, NY: Cornell University Library. http://historical.library.cornell.edu/IWP/index.html (2006)

OPEN COLLECTIONS PROGRAM: Women Working, 1800–1930 Cambridge, MA: Harvard University Library, Harvard University, http://ocp.hul.harvard.edu/ww/ (2006)

"In those good old days we used to have pantries and china closets and butteries and all that sort of thing, and people were contented."[1]
—*Eugene Field,* The House, *1896*